FROM WORRY
TO
WEALTHY

A Woman's Guide to Financial
Success Without the Stress

CHELLIE CAMPBELL

sourcebooks

Copyright © 2015 by Chellie Campbell
Cover and internal design © 2015 by Sourcebooks, Inc.
Cover design by Tom Mckeveny
Cover images © Bjorn Rune Lie, mstay/Getty Images

Sourcebooks and the colophon are registered trademarks of Sourcebooks, Inc.

Published by Sourcebooks, Inc.
P.O. Box 4410, Naperville, Illinois 60567-4410
(630) 961-3900
Fax: (630) 961-2168
www.sourcebooks.com

Library of Congress Cataloging-in-Publication data is on file with the publisher.

Printed and bound in the United States of America.
VP 10 9 8 7 6 5 4 3 2 1

Also by Chellie Campbell

The Wealthy Spirit

Zero to Zillionaire

To Nancy Sardella, CEO and founder of Women's Referral Service and Worthwhile Referral Sources.
A role model for all who do business according to her motto:
"Honestly, ethically, honorably, and with integrity."

Contents

Introduction
The Women's Game of Business: Making Money, Doing Good, and Having Fun

Do you feel that you're working too hard to pay your landlord, your credit card bills, and Uncle Sam with never enough left over for you?

Do you dream of having more income, money in the bank, and time off to travel?

Are your closest friends your electronic devices?

Are other people raising your children?

Is it a miracle if you get a massage?

You're not alone. So many women I meet love helping and serving others, but too often they leave their own good out of the equation, don't charge enough for their services, and give too much away for free. They don't like selling, because they've been turned off by too many "hard sell" tactics themselves and don't want to do that. They don't count their money because they haven't been shown how financial statements can help them grow, and money isn't their primary objective anyway. They work too hard at too many tasks and don't take enough time off to nurture themselves.

Psychologically, it takes enormous strength of character to face the fear of financial insecurity that a majority of women live with. An article in the *Los Angeles Times* by Walter Hamilton in March 2013 noted that "almost half of American women fear becoming bag ladies, even many of those earning six-figure salaries." Although six in ten women reported that they were the primary breadwinners and 54 percent of them managed the household finances, 49 percent of women feared becoming a homeless creature pushing a shopping cart, according to a poll by Allianz Life Insurance Company of North America.

Of the women surveyed who made more than $200,000 per year, more than a quarter of them were tortured by this fear of destitution! Kristina Walker, one of my licensed Financial Stress Reduction coaches, calls this the "bag lady syndrome."

The article went on to state that even though the women felt that they had "more earning power than ever before" and "handled major investment decisions," they worried that "financial achievement alienates both men and other women." Forty-two percent said "financially independent women intimidate men and run the risk of ending up alone." Thirty-one percent said "those women are hard to relate to and don't have many friends."

Yikes. Talk about a catch-22! If you're not financially successful, you'll end up homeless on the street, and if you are, no one will like you? Somehow we have to navigate through these conflicts to find both financial and personal success in the life we want to lead.

After all, what good is having a lot of money if you can't take time off to enjoy it? What good is having great Internet relationships if you don't have any time for in-person relationships with the ones you love the most—your family and best friends? Who wants to miss seeing the world, enjoying a scrumptious dinner at the Jules Verne in the Eiffel Tower, skiing in Vail, sailing in San Francisco Bay, birding in Cancun, eating a twenty-five-dollar ice-cream cone in Rome, winning a poker tournament on a Card Player Cruise to the Caribbean, or reading a zillion books just for the pleasure of it?

It isn't just about having the money—you have to make travel a goal. I never traveled at all until I noticed I was wishing I had. Now I've had all the adventures listed above because I put them on my agenda—and then on my calendar—for the past thirty years. **And you can too—I'll show you how in this book.**

So what do women—and the men who love them—need to do to change the social dynamics and cultural expectations about men and women, work and money? When I read about a Social Security Administration report on the savings habits of Americans that said that 29 percent of Americans died before reaching age sixty-five, and then after retiring at age sixty-five, 33 percent of them were dead within two years, I decided I wasn't going to wait until I retired to have a great life. I scaled my own speaking/writing/workshop career to include large amounts of time off to play. I don't overbook. I want to see a lot of white space in my calendar every week, because I learned that I don't have creative ideas in the middle of a too-busy appointment calendar and a too-full to-do list. I have creative ideas when I'm hiking, napping, driving, meditating, or getting a massage—when there's peace and quiet and time to think strategically.

I fell into financial coaching when I owned a business management firm for twelve years. Listening to my customers' needs for money management advice, I saw that no matter what their job, business, or level of income, people were stressed about money. I created the Financial Stress Reduction workshops, which I've now been teaching for more than twenty years, to help guide them to a richer and more fulfilling life—at work and at home.

I've worked with many women—and men too—who, like me, want to create a life while they're creating a living. They know that if you join the rat race, you'll just end up becoming a rat. As some-one said to me, "If they write the biography of your life in fourteen chapters, and thirteen of them are about work, it isn't going to have a happy ending."

If you want to play the game of "Who Has the Most Money," be my guest. But there's only one winner of that game, like in the *Highlander* movies and TV shows where "there can be only one." I always thought that premise was too stupid for words. Here were a bunch of immortals fighting and killing one another instead of banding together, toasting each other, and taking over the world.

What if they had instead channeled all that energy into making the world a better place for everyone? What if all the richest people in the world were doing that too? And I don't mean just donating to charity, but restructuring the game of business so more people benefit—not just women, but everyone?

Something is wrong with the game of business as it's currently being played. People are beginning to point out that the fracturing of the middle class and growing income inequality is a zero-sum game and is ultimately unsustainable. It's not okay that the rich-est eighty-five people have more money than the bottom half of humanity—3.5 billion people.

In Sam Polk's article "For the Love of Money," published in the *New York Times*, he wrote, "In my last year on Wall Street my bonus was $3.6 million—and I was angry because it wasn't big enough. I was 30 years old, had no children to raise, no debts to pay, no philanthropic goal in mind. I wanted more money for exactly the same reason an alcoholic needs another drink: I was addicted."

When no one is satisfied unless they're number one, everybody is working way too hard. I'd rather play the game "Everybody Wins and Is Happy!"

Is it really bad for business to pay decent salaries to your employees? Or to give equal pay for equal work? Provide medical insurance? Give compassionate leave for family emergencies? Share some of your profits with your workers? Have generous overtime and vacation pay? If you can't do that and still make good money, you have a bad business plan.

The balance sheet I care about is the happiness balance sheet, and I know a lot of women who are with me on that. We want flexible work hours, time off to take care of family emergencies, time to raise children and nurture families, time for hobbies, music, theater, dancing, travel, and seeing the world. We want compliments, testimonials, acknowledgments. We want to work with people we like, in an atmosphere of encouragement, joy, and laughter. We want to do good, feel good, and be good. We want our workplace to be a garden, not a prison.

Yes, we want to make money too, but we need to have a sense of what "enough money" is. Not everyone's goal is to lead a multibillion-dollar international conglomerate. If you want that, fine—that's wonderful, go for it! I honor and respect those women who have risen to the top and taken a seat at the big tables, like Sheryl Sandberg, the COO of Facebook and author of *Lean In: Women, Work, and the Will to Lead*.

But that's not what I want. I just want a seat at my own small table—and at the poker table on my day off.

It took a while for me to figure that out. Early in my working life, I read a book called *Games Mother Never Taught You* by Betty Lehan Harragan, which opened my eyes to the fact that business was a game run by men, and women weren't clued in to its rules. To play it and win, we were admonished to learn to "play like a man" and play "hardball."

"Winning isn't everything—it's the only thing" was first said by UCLA Coach Henry Russell Sanders, but Vince Lombardi repeated it often. Like many women back in the day before Title IX, I wasn't very involved in sports. I needed to learn that men treated business as a game to win, and that "it wasn't personal, it was business."

But it hurt and it felt personal when someone interrupted me at a meeting, spoke louder and more forcefully, and then took credit for my idea. It felt personal when I wasn't offered a promotion or a chance to grow and younger men were promoted above me and other women at work. I felt shut out when the company coed softball games were discontinued and all the men in the company joined a male-only softball league with the CEO.

So I studied the game of business, and much of what I learned was useful and good: how to negotiate better pay, market and sell products and services, use the power of networking, work with difficult people, read financial statements, handle competition, speak in public, hire and supervise others. I learned that it was important to leverage your talents and create multiple streams of residual income.

But the way the game is currently being played, not enough people are winning it. Too many people get stuck in low-paying and minimum-wage jobs, and too many of them are women. Add to that the reality that the best decisions for the bottom line are not always the best decisions for people. Ford Motor Company executives in the late '60s infamously calculated that it would be cheaper to pay out legal damages than to spend the money to fix design flaws that caused the Pinto's gas tank to explode in collisions.

When eighty-five people are winning and 3.5 billion people are losing, the game is broken. Throughout history, when that kind of disparity becomes too great, eventually the huge mass of people on the bottom revolt. A key element in the French Revolution was the gathering of the women of Paris who couldn't buy bread for their families. They had had enough. They marched on Versailles, took the king and queen prisoner, and that was the beginning of the end of royalty in France. Louis XV saw it coming when he famously said, "*Après moi, le déluge,*" but he didn't do anything to prevent it.

Of course I'm not suggesting that we're at that point—or at least, not here in the United States. There are a lot of revolutions happening around the world though, and at the bottom of it all is the economic disenfranchisement of huge swathes of people.

But I think we're ready to have a quiet revolution, one that changes the game, opens it to more players; where the rich aren't quite so rich and the poor aren't quite so poor, and most people are fat and happy in the middle. As former Labor Secretary Robert Reich said to David Lazarus of the *Los Angeles Times*, "When so much of the purchasing power, so much of the economic gain, goes to the very top, there's simply not enough purchasing power in the rest of the economy."

When I mentioned these ideas to one of my writer friends, Linda Sivertsen, she said, "But the company is responsible to its shareholders and they won't be happy if the stock price goes down." I replied, "That's because they're coming from the old paradigm that money is the only thing that matters to stockholders. Let those stockholders of the old order sell their shares and go elsewhere. Let the marketing for the new stockholders, who give weight to other values in addition to money, commence!"

Two minutes later, she emailed me a link to an online report about how Tim Cook, CEO of Apple, stood firm on their commitment to environmental initiatives and renewable energy sources. Certain conservative shareholders at a shareholders meeting argued that the company shouldn't be pursuing initiatives that didn't improve the company's bottom line. Cook responded that "we do a lot of things for reasons besides profit motive. We want to leave the world better than we found it." He said anyone who didn't agree should sell their shares and "get out of the stock."

I loved that! Big businesses can be conscious and game changing too. Change is coming, and women can help facilitate it.

Why should women—or men—continue to embrace the old

masculine model of success? And why is it still not okay for men to embrace more traditionally feminine goals? Why can't the game of business itself change to become more user- and family-friendly, more conciliatory, share more of the wealth, be more fun?

Instead of waiting for women to learn how to become more aggressive and take a seat at the table, leaders should *invite* women to the table. Not all talent comes in an aggressive package. Many women don't want success if it comes with the high price tag corporate America puts on it. Lynne Twist, in her book *The Soul of Money*, writes about speaking to a high-level group of female executives at Microsoft whose average net worth was $10 million. Although they were proud of their successes and honors in the company, they regretted that they put their families second and didn't take vacations. For most of them, "their life was their computer screen," and they thought that "someday they would retire and live happily ever after."

As I heard Terry Cole-Whittaker put it so succinctly years ago, "Someday is not a day of the week." You can't go back and enjoy your kids' childhoods after you retire.

It's time for us to argue for a change in the rules.

The Woman's Game of Business

Women love to do good work that helps people. They often put that at the forefront of their intentions when choosing their professions. More women are starting businesses, becoming freelancers, and choosing companies to work for with flexible schedules to create businesses that are more congenial for the people who work in them. When I woke up to the fact that I could make up a new game, play by my own rules, and decide for myself what winning is, I invented my speaking/writing/teaching business and found joy—and money—in helping others find joy and money. I love my life!

But we need to make money too. We can't just focus on the joy of the work and helping others and leave earning a good living out of the equation. Women often think it's greedy to charge too much money and then end up not charging enough. If you don't earn enough to sustain yourself and your family, how much help can you give the world?

If you want more joy in your business and more love in your life, want to do more good for more people, have more time off to play and nurture your families, and make more money at the same time, this book is for you. Its focus is on mastering the tools for financial success that will enable you to have the richest experience possible in your business and your personal life.

This book will address many of the issues women face when trying to make money, do good, have fun, and live a balanced life. How do you handle the stress of a career? What if you're climbing the ladder of success and need to take risks to get there? What if you're asked to join a new start-up company for less pay than you make now? What if you're asked to start a new division at your current company, but it's experimental and might fail?

What if you work for yourself—or want to? How do you handle the stresses of creating your income from scratch? How do you face erratic income as cash flow rises and falls? How much should you invest in yourself and your business? How do you qualify for loans to expand your business in the hope that you can generate more customers? How do you take time off to be with your family, take vacations, and nurture yourself when you're afraid you'll lose business whenever you aren't there?

How do you deal with the financial stress of it all?

Yes, and while you're doing all of that, you have to deal with the bane of every working woman: society's expectations of what's appropriate and "feminine" for a woman, from styles of communication to styles of clothing. The school system betrays everyone by keeping them in the dark about how to make money, negotiate salaries, and ask for what they want. Men get the message from our culture. Women are trained to wait for the man to ask them to the dance, for a date, to get married.

In school, if you do good work, turn it in on time, and obey the rules, you get an A and a gold star. Women graduate to the workplace and think it is going to be the same—that they will automatically be rewarded for doing a good job. That the powers that be will notice their contributions and shower them with raises, bonuses, and perks. They resent it bitterly when they discover that's not how it works. If and when they figure out they have to be more aggressive and ask for what they want, they get lambasted for being too masculine, forward, or bitchy.

How do you get support and understanding from the men in your life who also have expectations about women's roles? Are they excited about your advancing at work or going out on your own? Are they happy to see you go back to school to learn a new career? Or are they worried sick that you're going out on a limb? Do they help you with the housework? Or do they see the value in paying for housekeepers and cleaning services? Do you ask them for permission to spend money—even expenses you deem necessary? Do you give them veto power over your business activities? Do they show pride in your accomplishments and brag about them to your friends?

When my first book, *The Wealthy Spirit*, was released, my family got together for dinner to celebrate. I was excited to show them the finished product that I had been working on for nearly four years. As I passed around copies of the book and they exclaimed how beautiful it was and how excited they were for me, I mentioned how helpful my wonderful agent, Lisa Hagan, had been. My dad perked up at that and said, "Agent! That would be a good job for you!"

Oh, dear, I thought. *After all this time, he's still wishing I had a secure paycheck and a secure job.*

Dad was a child of the Depression, and he had always been

very supportive of my ventures—the Bank of Mom and Dad had helped me out a time or two when things got tough. That night I realized that I hadn't shared how good things had gotten and that I had been comfortably making a nice six-figure income for a number of years. So a week or two later, I purposefully mentioned that fact in a conversation, and he stopped short and looked at me with a smile of surprise and a lot of pride too. He never mentioned a job to me again.

Why had I neglected to mention my financial success before that? I was more comfortable asking him for advice about problems than bragging about my success, but that didn't give him a balanced picture of my business. I had to shift my thinking about that before I could change my conversations with my father.

So when I embarked upon writing this new book for women in business, I wanted to share tips for interacting with all the people in their lives, as well as strategies for financial success.

And maybe, while women and men work to change the game of business and our culture from one of competition and winner-take-all to one of consensus and everybody wins, we can give our attention and value to the creation of wealth beyond money. We can create richer, fuller, happier workplaces that benefit everyone.

Conscious Businesses Are Changing the Rules

It's already shifting. Some individuals and corporations are refocusing their business strategies, giving more benefits and higher salaries and bonuses, requiring less travel and fewer hours, implementing more family-friendly policies, and creating happier and more user-friendly workplaces.

Deloitte Touche Tohmatsu changed their policies to be more female-friendly to retain their female employees but found that men took advantage of the flexible work arrangements and less travel requirements and were happier too. Tom's Shoes donates a pair of shoes for every pair purchased. They send their executives on "giving trips" to donate shoes that have been customized for the terrain of the country they're in. Jill Waters, marketing director for Right At Home, a company that provides in-home care and assistance, shared with me that her boss, Tammy Weddle, allows her to volunteer up to eight hours of company time a week "because she believes in giving back to the community she serves." From the decision to donate 1 percent of sales to progressive environmental groups to giving his employees flextime, Yvon Chouinard's philosophy for Patagonia in *Let My People Go Surfing* helps his customers, his employees, and the world.

The Shine Law Firm of Australia is proactive at hiring female attorneys. Simon Morrison, the managing director, told me that they discovered that the women they hired were better at mediation and litigation than the men, so it became a profitable business strategy for them to figure out what women wanted in the workplace. When the single women got married and started having children, they didn't want to work as many hours, so the firm designed flexible work hours to suit them. They also released a generous parental program, which included a significant contribution toward the cost of child care.

Jodie Willey protested when they asked her to become the CEO of the company. She was planning to start a family, she told them. "So what?" they answered. "If you need more time off for that, you can have it." She accepted the position and told me the atmosphere of the company was one that creates confidence, rewards and recognizes competence, and helps women grow professionally and personally.

Let's make that the new standard in the marketplace.

We need men and women to combine their strengths to change the way "business as usual" is done, to share the load and share the rewards. Yes, let us be proud of our bottom lines, but let us be equally proud of how we produced them, that we did so in an enlightened way, serving our employees, associates, partners, children, families, and communities, as well as our customers and stockholders.

In early 2014, Maria Shriver, in partnership with the Center for American Progress, released *The Shriver Report: A Woman's Nation Pushes Back from the Brink* in which she outlined some of the causes of the fact that nearly a third of all women in America are living on the brink of poverty. The main reason, she writes, is that the American political, economic, social, religious, and cultural systems have not caught up with the reality of women's lives.

Today, only 20 percent of American families have a male bread-winner and a female homemaker. According to a Pew Research Center report, 28 percent of American children are being raised by stay-at-home mothers. That figure was 48 percent in 1970. "What women need now is a country that supports the reality of women's dual roles as by far the majority of the nation's caregivers and bread-winners," Shriver says in the report. Raising the standard of living benefits the entire community.

Let's all work together to redefine success so it isn't just about the money, fame, glory, stock price, fast cars, beautiful companions, and the race to be number one. Let success be measured by how much good you do in the world, how much compassion you have for others, how happy and fulfilled your employees are, how happy and fulfilled your families are, and how much great work you're able to do in just thirty to forty hours a week.

More women are making that choice today, starting businesses, becoming freelancers, and doing great work in the world on their own terms. They are creating a living but creating a life at the same time, successfully and happily, with time for their families, travel, play, enjoyment, and giving back. They have values and vision. What they need more is a voice.

I want to help women celebrate that they are creating a more user-friendly kind of business. That each one of them going it alone is not really alone but part of a larger collective of people who think business should always be ethical, fair, and rewarding to both their customers and themselves.

I'm advocating not only a woman-friendly workplace, but also a people-friendly workplace. Many men want these values too. Working together, enlightened businesses can create a world where everyone has enough. Instead of "winner take all," we can create a world where "winner shares all" and everybody wins.

It begins with you—your inspiration, your commitment to excellence, your desire to help others through your chosen profession. When you're happy and fulfilled and prosperous, you are an example to all the women around you who want those things too. They are looking to you for the answers regarding how to have them.

Live your dream, go for your goals, and take plenty of time off to love your family and friends. You can stop worrying about becoming a bag lady. You can have a wonderful life and plenty of time and money with which to live it. I want to watch you do it, and I wrote this book to help you get there.

You are the change we all want to see in the world and you can do it!

Confidence, Charisma, Clients, Credentials, Competition, and Cash

Successful women are confident. The brighter that confidence shines, the more people say they have charisma. The more charisma they have, the more clients they attract. They don't worry about credentials or competition, because they know they are unique and no one can copy who they are. This is the mind-set you need to have if you want to bring in the cash.

Some people are offended by that, but it isn't said in arrogance. There's an important secret ingredient that must be included in the mix, and women are naturally fabulous at it: caring about others.

In this chapter, I'll show you how to balance confidence with caring, appreciate your own true talents, and let your charismatic light shine!

Confidence

"Besides which, you see, I have confidence in me!"

—Julie Andrews as Maria in *The Sound of Music*, Rodgers and Hammerstein

Her song was of course followed by a whispered, "Oh, help," when she arrived at the gates of the mansion where she was to be the nanny to the captain's children…

Isn't that often the way of it? We bolster ourselves with good thoughts and fine intentions, and then our hearts sink when we encounter the realities that face us. When we set out to find our own way in the world, to invent a career for ourselves or start our own business, the first obstacle we face is internal.

It takes courage to become a freelance writer, invent a seminar, or decide to go it alone as an attorney, chiropractor, nutritionist, travel agent, salesperson, or any other professional who embarks on the journey of creating their own living. To move up the ladder in a corporate environment does too—you have to be willing to stand out and ask for promotions and raises. You have to have confidence in your abilities, not only professionally, but also in being able to master sales and marketing, attract the clients you want, and negotiate enough money to pay your bills.

It takes courage to take that risk. And to take it, you have to believe in yourself. You must have some of that already, or you wouldn't have started down this path. You must have already helped some people and gotten good results and feedback. Don't you have supporters who cheer you on? The first important step is for you to believe in their good opinion of you.

Focus on what you can do, what's working, your skills and talents, and on everything good about yourself and your abilities. You are terrific, fabulous, and wonderful, and you deserve to win!

Eek.

If that thought seems arrogant or immodest, it might be because it contradicts the "nice girl" mind-set that's been drilled into us for years. Many studies have shown that women are much more likely to be self-critical than men. And we think it's a good thing.

Would you want to hire an attorney who modestly claims they're "okay" at their job? Thinking positively about yourself is going to get you farther along the road to success than focusing on your collection of worries, fears, doubts, and insecurities will.

Do you know that there are people out there praying for you to show up?

It's true. There are people who need you. They need what you have to offer and they don't know where you are. So you have to stand up and stand out. You need to show them you have confidence in yourself so that they can have confidence in you. When they hire you, they are going to be over the moon that they found you. And they will praise you and pay you for helping them!

With confidence, you can give yourself permission to make a lot of money. More than you're making now. To do that you need to clear away the barriers to your success—internal and external. Set the intention now that you are going to maximize your potential so that you can create a great income for yourself helping the people you were born to help.

People love confidence. Not arrogance—that's too much. Not nervousness—that's too little. People who are nervous don't go to networking meetings, or they sit at the back if they do. They don't give speeches, volunteer to be president of the club, or even introduce themselves when given the opportunity.

Just the right amount of confidence is a mixture of feeling blessed that you're able to do what you do, grateful that you're allowed to do it, and happy to help others with it. You don't have to know everything, and you don't have to be the best one in the world—you just have to help the people who come to you so they can get what they need. "Your message is medicine for the world and you were chosen to deliver it," as business and life coach Nancy Marmolejo so eloquently put it.

You'll get everything you want if you listen to the right voice in your head—the one that says, "I am fabulous and people love to give me money!" Not the one that says, "I can't afford to make a mistake so I'd better not say anything." The first voice will put a smile on your face and the second one, a frown. Which face do you think will attract the people you want to work with?

There was a time when I didn't have any confidence and I really wished I did. When I started my Financial Stress Reduction workshops, I had no brand, no book, no certification, and no reputation. Nobody knew who I was, why I was teaching workshops, or what "financial stress reduction" meant—but it sounded good and people needed it. I knew I had some tools and strategies that could help. So I created my own brand and reputation and certified myself.

But I was nervous meeting people at networking events, and my knees shook whenever I spoke to a group. People visibly withdrew when I introduced myself and quickly excused themselves to go talk with someone else. As a former musical comedy actress, I knew I was losing my audience. But what was wrong? What did I need to do to stop repelling people and start attracting them?

Finally, one night, I gave a speech to about one hundred women. My nerves were getting the best of me, and my focus was all on me. *Me.* But as I reached the podium and looked out at the audience, I saw a woman who was leaning forward, looking worried but hopeful. She had come to hear how to reduce her financial stress. As I quickly looked at a couple of other people who wore similar expressions, I realized that this talk wasn't about me at all. It was about helping them! And I could do it!

I said a quick prayer: "God, please put the words in my mouth that need to be heard today to help somebody." I felt all my nervousness drain out of my body. I spoke powerfully, like I had never done before. Words flowed and I never looked at my notes once. At the end, I got a big round of applause, and a lot of people came up to talk with me. That was in 1991, and I have said that prayer every day since then.

It still makes me chuckle when people say, "Oh, it's easy for you,

Chellie—you're a natural." Like isn't it just easier to believe that people were *born* with skills and talents rather than acknowledge that they had to *work* to get them? Because if it's some special gift people are born with, you can just relax and say, "Well, they were born like that and I wasn't, so I don't have to try to be that."

I once gave a short speech of about ten minutes to five hundred people. It went really well, and I got some lovely applause. Afterward, one of my friends came up to me and congratulated me.

"Chellie, that was a wonderful speech."

"Thank you so much," I replied.

"Can I ask you a question?" she said.

"Sure, what?"

"Did you practice it?" she asked.

I stared at her incredulously. "Of course I did!" I said. "What do you think—it all just came pouring out unwritten and unrehearsed? I spent hours writing it, and I practiced it every day in the mirror, in the car, before I went to bed, and when I woke up!"

She grimaced, said, "I was afraid you were going to say that," and walked away.

Nope, I wasn't born knowing how to do it. I worked at it. So the bad news is that you are going to have to do some work to develop confidence and charisma. Why is that surprising? You had to work to become good at your job, didn't you?

The good news is that when you study and practice and learn this, you will feel great and do great at presenting yourself to others. It will take some time and it will take some practice, but you will get better every time. And then, when they say, "Oh, it's easy for you—you're a natural!" you'll laugh just like I do.

Charisma: The "It" Factor

Charisma comes from confidence. That's what we respond to when we enjoy a song, a performance, a speech, or someone whose caring for us through their work makes us feel special. Some people love what they are doing so much their joy spills over onto you and you both are better as a result.

Notice what happens in the singing competitions on television. All the judges are clearly looking not only for great singers, but also those with the likability factor. Even if they are really talented singers, they aren't going to make it if they don't have charisma.

But you can tell who has "It" too, can't you? It's written on their faces, in their body language, and in their energy. You can feel it. They love what they're doing and they love it if you love it too.

This is the secret that the winners of the singing competitions know:

1. They know they are *good* at what they do.
2. They *love* doing it.
3. They *show* that they love it.
4. They have *fun* doing it.
5. They *connect* personally with the audience and invite them to have fun too.
6. Their performances are for *themselves* and the *people who love them* and nobody else counts.

One of the best examples I ever saw of a professional singer engaging the audience was a recent performance by Paul Anka at the Pechanga Resort and Casino. Yes, the 1950s teen idol is still rocking it onstage. My buddies and I thought it would be a hoot, so we got tickets.

Paul entered the theater through the aisles while singing one of his big '50s hits, "Diana." He was all smiles, supercharged with energy, greeting audience members, shaking hands, dancing with a woman, and when some latecomers came in, he guided them to their seats and changed the words to the song to welcome them and tell them it was okay they were late. You could tell instantly that he was thoroughly enjoying himself.

When he got onstage, he said a big "Hello!" to everyone, then said, "You know how they tell you that you can't take pictures or videos here?" Everyone nodded and answered yes, and he said, "Well, I don't care about that. Take all the pictures you want!" The crowd roared and took out their cell phones as he started his next song.

A woman in the second row started talking on her cell phone, so he came down from the stage and said, "Who are you talking to?" I couldn't hear what she said, but he said, "Give me the phone," which she did. He then started singing to the person on the phone! He changed the lyrics, singing, "Yes, it's really me. Yes, I'm singing to you!" It was hysterical.

He had the audience in the palm of his hand within the first ten minutes of his show, and we never left it. What charm! And it was all because he loved what he was doing and he loved us because we were there loving it too. Magic.

That's charisma.

Now, you may not be a singer or ever want to be on *American Idol*, *The Voice*, *X Factor*, or whatever. But wouldn't you like to be a star in your field? How would your life change if your personal presence was so magnetic that people were clamoring to work with you?

It's a technique that can be learned. Marilyn Monroe could turn on charisma in an instant. In her book *Marilyn and Me*, Susan Strasberg told how she and Marilyn were walking down the street in New York and no one was paying them any attention. When she mentioned it, Marilyn turned to her and said, "Oh, you want to see me be *her*?"

Marilyn straightened up, threw her head back, and started smiling at people. Immediately, people started to stare, point, and rushed to surround the star!

Now, I'm not saying you should try to be Marilyn. Trying to copy someone else is the biggest mistake you can make. But you can turn heads with your own brand of charisma and attract the people who need and want and who can benefit from what you have to offer. And get paid—*really well!*—for doing what you love!

Here's how it works.

Discover Your Talent

Everyone has something they excel at. Figure out what you have a natural inclination for and work to perfect that. Don't try out for a singing contest if you can't carry a tune, but maybe comedy would work. If you don't like being onstage but love designing clothes, you could be a costumer. If you're a good friend and listener, you could be a coach or a therapist. You were born talented at something, but often it seems so natural to you that you might not recognize it. Make a list of all your talents, then ask a friend to make a list of what they think your talents are. You might be surprised at the results.

When I became a bookkeeper and business manager, I thought it was so simple that everyone could do it. It took me a long time to see it was an innate talent that not everyone had. One of the games my sisters and I played when we were kids was "business." Jane owned the restaurant and made sandwiches, Carole owned the beauty salon and did our hair and makeup, and I played accountant with bunches of receipts I had dredged up from the trash. So it's not such a surprise I later owned a bookkeeping service.

Practice Being Confident

You must have confidence in yourself and your ability in order to succeed. A few people are born with confidence or develop it early. For most of us, though, it takes hiring a coach, taking lessons, learning positive thinking, and lots of practice. Malcolm Gladwell in his book *Outliers: The Story of Success* estimates that it takes ten thousand hours or ten years to become great at anything. So don't give up before you get there.

How do you get confidence if you're insecure? Act as if you are confident. Practice, study, practice, learn, fall down, get up, and practice again. Eventually, you will realize that all your insecurity is just an illusion. As Dan Zadra said, "Worry is a misuse of imagination." You can just as easily imagine that you're fabulous. If you don't think so, then you have been listening to the wrong little inner voice. It took me a while to gain confidence in myself. I finally discovered it when I was selected to be in a summer stock company at the University of Oregon. The first day, we had to sing a song in front of all the directors. When I started worrying about that, a little voice inside me said, "Go for broke. You don't know any of these people, and after this summer, you'll never see them again. Sing out loud and strong. Have fun with it and they'll have fun with you." I sang like I had never sung before, and the director of one of the musicals walked onstage, took my hand, and gave me the script for the lead in *Celebration*. I had never played a leading role before.

With experience, you become proficient at your talent and appreciate what you can do. With that comes more and more enjoyment as you do it, and then you trust yourself to do it well. You'll then expect other people to like it too, and some of them will. They will compliment and enjoy your work, and that will make you even more confident.

Share Your Talent with Love

This is the "It." When your love and joy at what you're doing overflows, it shows on your face and in your body language. Humans are social animals—it is natural for you to want to communicate and share your joy with others. The key is to love your audience, customers, or clients and invite them in to enjoy with you.

Years ago, I saw a man seem to lose his place in the middle of giving a speech. He looked down at his papers and was silent. The tension in the room rose. It was very uncomfortable! After a full minute of silence, he looked up and smiled and said, "You were all pulling for me, weren't you?" It was a great lesson: the audience wants you to do well. Your customers and clients want you to do well. They want to enjoy the ride with you. Trust them and take them with you. Have fun!

And that's what brings in the cash too.

Be Proud of Your Looks

We want to shine, to show our best selves, to get compliments. We want to look gorgeous, talented, and successful.

This is an especially difficult subject for women. The overemphasis on appearance is more detrimental to girls than boys because of the way women are portrayed in the male-dominated media as being more valued for being beautiful than for being smart or talented. When you watch television shows, especially shows with a number of young twentysomethings, how many of them are unattractive? Not many. The daily media barrage gives us a distorted picture of what the real world actually looks like.

Many studies have documented a severe drop in self-esteem in young girls that happens between the ages of twelve and seventeen. A report from the *Journal of Research on Adolescence* stated that a lot of the responsibility for this lies with the fact that perceptions of appearance and self-worth are linked. "The media—magazines, TV, films, advertising, music videos—not only emphasize that female self-worth should be based on appearance, but also present a powerful cultural ideal of female beauty that is becoming increasingly unattainable (Richins, 1991; Silverstein, Perdue, Peterson, & Kelly, 1986). For example, a recent content analysis of TV sitcoms found that 76% of female characters were below average weight (Fouts & Burggraf, 2000)."

But look around you as you walk down the street or shop at a grocery store. Most of the people you see are average in appearance. Many people who aren't beautiful stand out. They have an energy, a charisma beyond their looks. They smile at you and nod. They'll ask, "How are you?" and wait for your answer. They look genuinely interested because they are interested. They are engaged with you.

It's been said of President Bill Clinton that when he spoke with you, he made you feel like you were the only person in the room. People love that kind of attention. It won't matter what you look like. The ability to genuinely like people and engage them trumps beauty every time. And yes, you can learn this—inner beauty is within everyone's grasp. Reach inward to develop it and reach outward to perfect it. Be somebody who lights up the room, not someone who dampens it. You are your own walking advertisement for your products and services, and people will remember more about how they felt around you than how you looked. A smile is still the best face-lift there is.

Clients

You have to give up trying to be perfect and appeal to everyone. You can't be all things to all people. Trying to please everyone is a losing strategy.

Did you ever take a sales training course where they taught you how to try to appeal to everyone? I did. They would divide people into four quadrants; quadrant one was the conservative group—I call them the blue suit people. They told me that to appeal to them, I would have to speak slowly and softly, give them lots of facts and figures, wear a "dress for success" blue suit, not talk with my hands, and be reserved in my behavior. Then for the quadrant two people—the more extroverted, "outside the box" people—I would need to dress more creatively, tell jokes and stories, and not use too many facts and figures. Quadrants three and four were other types, with different dress codes and behaviors that would attract them.

Isn't that just crazy?

That might be fine psychology if you are meeting one-on-one with someone to purchase a product and you're never going to see them again, but what do you do if you're going to work with them in a personal service business? Or with a group?

I'll tell you what most people do—they become bland and boring. They don't let their true selves show. They try to give a little bit of everything so they appeal to everybody, and they end up appealing to nobody.

Let me give you a tip: hiding your true self never works for very long. You aren't going to attract your favorite clients, your best friends, or the partner of your dreams if you don't show your personality and who you really are.

So many times, we are afraid to be real, to show our true inner being, to be vulnerable and stand in all our perfection and imperfection in front of another person. We try to figure out what they want to see or hear and then struggle to be that and say that. So many dating books revolve around planning and strategies, and "say this" and "don't say that," and "what a man wants is" and "what a woman wants is," but none of that measures up to being your true self. Be authentically who you are and say what you think and show your feelings. What could you possibly gain by hiding yourself? Showing a fake self can only result in a fake relationship. Those who cannot measure up to your truth don't deserve it.

Those who remain will be your best clients for life.

Choose Clients You Love

Think about this: How many clients do you really need?

It was a really important moment in my life when I figured out that I only needed eighty clients to take my workshop each year. There are around twenty million people in the greater Los Angeles area, so I know I'm not going to run out of people. Since my books *The Wealthy Spirit* and *Zero to Zillionaire* have been published all over the world and I started teaching my classes as teleclasses, my potential client base numbers in the millions. But I still only need eighty.

I get to work with just a few select clients of my choosing. They will be fabulous, gifted, and creative. They will be smart, clever, and fun, and they will love me just the way I am in the same way I love them just the way they are! Because I'm going to say no to everyone who isn't like that.

Do you see how freeing this concept is? You don't ever have to work with an angry, awful person who doesn't want to pay you what you're worth. The only reason anyone does that is because they are afraid there isn't a fabulous, wonderful person itching to work with them and pay them big bucks just around the corner.

But there is. And every awful client you say yes to today keeps you from meeting the fabulous client tomorrow.

Enjoy Being Yourself

So who are you? It might help to choose a category that suits you best—you might be a romantic leading lady like a relationship coach or couples therapist, or the comic best friend who designs humorous websites or writes creative blogs. Perhaps earth mother is your niche, and you give people massages or teach them yoga. Maybe you're a techno geek and do amazing technical wizardry.

Once you figure out your basic character, list your special qualities, quirks, and knowledge that make you stand out. Show your personality in your style of dress, your marketing materials, what you say, and everything you do. You only want to attract people who like who you really are.

The best piece of marketing advice I ever got was from Gene

Call's Word of Mouth marketing seminar: "You want to *attract* the people you want and *repel* the people you don't want."

I was shocked. No one ever told me in any way shape or form that I should repel people. I was brought up to be a "good girl" and be pleasing and pleasant to everyone.

Like that's even possible. The only way you can do that is if you have no personality.

When I started running with that idea, climbing out of the "good girl box" and showing my real self in all my colors, I started introducing myself as a financial stress reducer who treated money disorders—spending bulimia and income anorexia. I sang bits in my thirty-second commercials, like "You're going to be rich tomorrow" to the tune from *Annie*. I started wearing gold tennis shoes everywhere I went—it's part of my brand. I did the quadrant two, wild-and-crazy-girl me, regardless of how other people were going to react, because as Terry Cole-Whittaker says, "What you think of me is none of my business."

Darlene Basch, a marriage and family therapist, has an earth mother presence. She begins her introduction with a beautiful smile and a slow, mellow "Welcome to the world of calm," and everyone sighs with her. Kay Rodine, an interior designer, shows her perky comic best friend personality when she asks the audience, "What would your house say to you if it could?" And everyone who knows her answers, "Don't move! Redecorate!" A sophisticated romantic leading lady type, the owner of Cash Flow Services says, "A machine that makes money can be legal, just call Evelyn Siegel." Marc Chroman, techno geek extraordinaire, asks, "What's the most important thing about computers? Backup, backup, backup!" They all match the marketing styles of their businesses to their personalities.

Our job is to be authentically who we are, and we will attract the people who like people like us. It's only when you are real that

I have the possibility to get to know you, like you, trust you—and only then will I buy from you. Anything else is false advertising.

Appeal to "Your People"

There are two groups of people in life: "your people" and "not your people." Your people like you immediately; they smile, draw closer, and ask you questions. Not your people have out-of-body experiences around you. (I believe in out-of-body experiences because I've seen them happen: the person draws back, their eyes glaze over, and you know they just left the room.)

Have you ever attracted "not your people" as clients or business associates and had a terrible time working with them? They criticize you, they're never happy, they always ask for things to be redone, and they don't give you any compliments. And then on top of that, they often don't want to pay your fee! It's painful and hard to work with people who are never going to like and appreciate you no matter what you do.

Design your brand to let your true self shine through, and then "your people" are going to flock to you in droves!

Get Used to Rejection

The biggest problem in having confidence is not getting bent out of shape and falling into a quivering mass of jelly when somebody tells you no.

Actually, you need to thank all those "not your people" for getting out of your way fast and preventing you from wasting your time and your glorious self on them. Every time one of them walks away, quits your program, unsubscribes from your list, or tells you they don't like you or what you say, they are doing you a big favor. They are getting out of the way and moving you closer to finding "your people."

One of the best sales demonstrations I ever witnessed was a

seminar leader who went around to the members of the audience, who had coffee cups, with a pot of coffee. He said to each one, "Would you like more coffee?" Some said, "Yes, please," and held out their cups and he'd pour them some coffee. Others said, "No thanks," and he went on to the next person.

When he got back to the front of the room, he said, "This is what sales is all about. The waitress at Denny's is just looking for the people who want more coffee and helping them to have it. But when someone doesn't want more coffee, she doesn't go back to the kitchen and cry about it: 'What did I do wrong? Did I say the wrong thing? Is my apron dirty? Don't they like blonds? Do I need to work on my accent? Isn't the coffee any good? Oh, I never do anything right!'"

Do you do that when someone blasts your ideas on your blog? Or calls you up and says your email was all wrong? Or unsubscribes from your list?

Stop that. You are beautiful, talented, and creative. You want to help people and you do. Lead with that. Collect evidence in testimonials, praise, and compliments from "your people" and read them whenever anyone is mean or rejects you. If you read a couple of my one-star horrible reviews of *Zero to Zillionaire* on Amazon.com, you'll know I've had to follow my own advice. You can join me in playing that great Taylor Swift song, "Mean," which she wrote about a critic who had blasted her in print, and laugh.

Credentials

Some people need to have credentials to feel confident. I think people tend to make too much out of credentials. It's all very well to go to school, get a degree, and set up a professional practice. It means that you have accomplished a certain amount of study and discipline, and that's great. Certainly you want a doctor or an attorney with good credentials.

But there are a great many career paths that don't depend on having an official educational credential. Bill Gates of Microsoft, Steve Jobs of Apple, and Steven Spielberg of Dreamworks, for example. They were born with talents, skills, and creativity and went off on their own without getting a college degree or any certification. They just went to work and started *doing* it.

Once at a networking meeting I attended, each person took their turn giving their thirty-second commercial about their business. Three people who gave their presentations right before me put emphasis on their credentials and certifications—one had a master's degree in business, one had a license in marriage and family therapy (LMFT), and one had a PhD.

Then it was my turn. "I acknowledge these wonderful people who have such distinguished degrees," I began, then turned to the audience and smiled. "I, on the other hand, have no credentials whatsoever. I'm a graduate of MSU—Make Stuff Up. I'm a financial stress reducer, and I certified myself!"

Not only did I get a good laugh and some warm smiles, but a bunch of people also came up to me afterward to get to know me. Just "my people." The people who want credentials went to the other people. Perfect.

Back in the day before the proliferation of colleges and universities that everyone could attend, most people learned a trade or profession by becoming an apprentice to a master craftsman or tradesperson. You worked your way up to journeyman and then became a master yourself. We tend to forget that there's more than one way to become proficient at something.

In the twenty-plus years I've been teaching and writing about finance, I've only been asked for my credentials one time. A woman had already signed up for my class when a friend asked her what my credentials were. "I don't know!" she exclaimed and called me to find out.

I laughed. "Well, I have a bachelor's degree in dramatic art and belong to the Screen Actors Guild and Actors Equity, which qualifies me as a speaker," I told her, "and I owned a business management firm with thirteen employees for twelve years, which gave me a lot of experience with helping people manage their finances. But my true credentials are the results my clients get."

In the end, it's the results that count. When you buy a painting, do you care what degrees the artist had? No. You just care that you think the painting is so beautiful that you want to own it and hang it in your house.

Competition

It's hard to have confidence in the face of competition, like the singers on *American Idol* or any of us who are competing for contracts or clients. For some time, I was really jealous of Suze Orman. One night, in one of my workshops, I made a comment about how she had beat me onto the *Oprah* show, and I wasn't pleased. A man in the class set me straight right away: "You should be thanking Suze. She's proved there's a market for what you do!"

I stopped and looked at him and cocked my head. "You know, I never thought about it that way before. You're right! I should be glad she's out there blazing the trail and making it easier for the rest of us female financial educators to have credibility and be taken seriously. Thank you for sharing that!"

There was a conversation I joined in on Facebook a while ago, started by Karyn Greenstreet, a terrific business coach. A few people mentioned how they felt it was hard for them to be in business because there was so much competition. Here's what they said:

> *No! No! No! I got an email from a student today who said she wasn't going to launch her class because she found out that a competitor had a similar class. There is abundance all around*

us, and you will draw the right students to your class not just because of WHAT you teach, but WHO the teacher is (you!). Do not give up on your dream just because someone else has the same idea.

Who cares that someone else is doing something similar; similar is not the same, it cannot be the same… Each person has their own process they take people through and it will never be the same as someone else's.

A friend recently told me that if many people are teaching the same topic you're passionate about, it doesn't mean you shouldn't do it. It means that topic is so important that it needs more than one messenger.

And I think this comment from Karyn was the capper:

I was just thinking: Can you imagine if the folks who wrote "West Side Story" said, "Oh, someone's already done this story. Let's not do it. There's too much competition with that Shakespeare feller." LOL

It was wonderful to see how many people chimed in to say that each person is unique and wonderful with gifts to share that will be needed by the very people who find them and hire them. Getting this kind of feedback and support from your peers is one of the best business uses of Facebook and other social media.

So what has "the competition" stopped you from doing?

You may not have the most beautiful voice, or the loudest, or the most melodic. But you have a voice that a few are attuned to so closely that it is the only one they can hear. Don't despair if others have more followers or more money or fame or glory—those are things of the world that don't always bring happiness to their owners. Revel in the joy you have and the joy you bring to others. Don't waste your time on the thought that you aren't the biggest or the best. How many are given that? Know that your life has beauty and purpose and be about your work, honestly and honorably, in gratitude for your gifts that you share with whatever part of the world is yours to touch.

Yes, you might be thinking, but then what do you *do*?

Nothing makes us doubt ourselves more than being confronted with the competition. You and your business could be humming along for years, fat and happy, and then someone else shows up doing the same thing. And cheaper! Or suddenly the new guy in the sales department is bringing in more business than you. Or a big department store opens near your little boutique.

And maybe then some of your clients go running off to sample the wares the competition is offering. I know during the last recession, there were suddenly a zillion money coaches, therapists, and consultants offering seminars and teleclasses on how to make more money.

So what do you do then?

I need "my people" to help me stay balanced. At one point, I was annoyed because I was feeling like other people were copying my writings and teachings and then sending out their own twists to what I said to market their own seminars and teleclasses. I spend a lot of time writing newsletters and various informative emails and blog posts. So I was in a bit of a snit over this.

In a monthly mastermind group with several other coaches, I mentioned this issue with some irritation. Louise Crooks asked, "What is it taking away from you?"

That stopped me in my tracks. "Uh..." I hesitated, thinking furiously. Maybe I was afraid I was losing business? People were going to other workshops instead of mine? But then I realized that

I lose nothing when other people get ideas from my work. Haven't I learned and gotten ideas from other teachers I've studied with and other great books I've read?

"Oh, Louise," I said, "thank you for that. I see clearly that I lose nothing from other people playing off my ideas. I have plenty of clients and I can only work with about eighty people a year. There's plenty of business for everyone!" I knew that. I just forgot for a minute.

There was general agreement about this, and Louise told us about a great book she was reading, *Steal Like an Artist: 10 Things Nobody Told You About Being Creative* by Austin Kleon, which I promptly purchased. It's terrifically funny, and enlightening too.

And Finally—Cash!

But then there's the next problem—I see a lot of people who have confidence and charisma and are entertaining, friendly, and fun to be with, but they aren't making any money.

They have a twelve-week program and charge forty dollars for it. Somehow they got the idea that they needed to make their program "affordable." Well, great, but when they do that, they can't afford anything themselves because they didn't make enough money to live on.

You can love yourself, develop your brand, make fabulous introductions, create a wonderful blog and newsletter, attract all the perfect clients you want, network and make lots of connections, give speeches to tremendous applause and acknowledgments, and create a name for yourself and stand out in your community. You can have all the confidence in the world, project perfect charisma, and attract the clients you love.

But if you don't learn the truth about money, you won't ever get the cash you want. You won't be able to ask them for the money. Or you won't charge them enough to make a good living. And what about an excellent living? A six-figure income? More?

Without this piece, you're going to leave buckets of cash on the floor everywhere you go. If you want to make more money, you need to know that the real money you lose in life is the money you fail to earn. The solution to that problem is in the next chapter.

The Real Money You Lose in Life Is the Money You Fail to Earn

"A scientific study did a demonstration showing that high-priced placebos, or sugar pills, are more effective than low-priced placebos."
—Notice in *Reader's Digest*

There is one attitude that will kill your business faster than any other—"I don't care about the money."

I laugh when I read that, but I know in my heart it is true. People hold things that cost more money in higher esteem. If you go to the furniture store and see one couch for $500 and another for $1500, which one do you think is a better couch?

It just seems natural that if it costs more, it's worth more. But that's not necessarily the case. If the first couch was made by a woman and the second one was made by a man, they could actually be the same couch. Because across the board, women price themselves, their talents, abilities, and work lower than men do.

This is well-known, and businesses often take advantage of it.

Did you know that salespeople in car dealerships consistently quote higher prices to women than to men? Or that employers often make lower first offers to women than they make to men and take it for granted that women will work for less? Or that they routinely set higher targets against women, make tougher first offers, press harder for concessions, and resist conceding more than they would if they were negotiating with men?

In *Women Don't Ask: The High Cost of Avoiding Negotiation—and Positive Strategies for Change*, Linda Babcock and Sara Laschever revealed their studies showed that:

- Men think of negotiating as "winning a ballgame."
- Women think of negotiating as "going to the dentist."
- When men negotiate, they get paid approximately 30 percent more than women.
- By failing to negotiate their starting salary, a person can lose $500,000 by age sixty.

All of this results in women earning less than men from the day they first accept a job at a lower rate because they didn't negotiate to the day they retire on less savings, less Social Security, and less in whatever retirement account they managed to put together.

We have to learn to ask for more money and not settle for less than we deserve. We have to say no to salaries that are not commensurate with our talents, skills, and education. We have to say no to clients who don't want to pay us the fees we're worth.

Don't worry, I'm not going to teach you how to be overly aggressive, or demanding, or hard, or tough in any masculine way. If you tried that, it would likely backfire. Society has differing gender norms for men and women, so strong men are described as "take-charge types and leaders" while strong women are described as "bossy, confident, and aggressive." There is hope that this is changing. Sheryl Sandberg and other successful women are advocating for girls to be praised for their leadership skills instead of being called bossy. But the standard up until now has been that men are expected to be powerful, success-oriented, and in control. Women are expected to be nice, relationship-oriented, and helpful.

Perhaps women are naturally nice and great at caring about others. I think it might be partly biological—a woman needs to be able to put others first to raise children. Women are extremely adept at negotiating in one particular arena—they are great at asking on behalf of others. This giving quality makes us great caregivers, nurturers, teachers, and workers in the helping professions, especially in nonprofits.

Women are great at asking for:

- Charity
- Free stuff
- Discounts
- Barter
- Anything on behalf of children

We can sell our kids' candy bars and Girl Scout cookies like there's no tomorrow, put on a nonprofit event and fill the room, and go to the sales on Black Friday and fight for the items we want. But our client rosters stay thin and filled with people paying discounted rates—because they need us and want us and we want to help. We're so happy to have somebody say yes because that means we can stop marketing and selling!

There's the rub. As Stuart Wilde, author of *The Trick to Money Is Having Some!*, wrote, "In any business, there are jobs that are productive and sometimes confrontational, for they test you. And then there is all the other work, none of which earns any money."

This causes us difficulties when we need to earn a living. Women often tell me that they'd work for free if they didn't have any bills to pay. We naturally think of others and the stress they might have in paying us. So we make allowances, reduce our rate, and even give our work away for free. We send another email or write another blog post because it's less confrontational. We wait for people to call us because we don't want to bother them, even when they ask us to call them!

Heidi Parr Kerner, a smart and savvy marketing consultant, told me she went to a networking meeting and told two people she wanted to buy their products and services. "Oh, I need your products!" she said to the woman who was a skin-care representative. "Please call me tomorrow morning so I can talk with you about what I need to buy."

Then she saw a woman who did graphic design. "Oh, I need graphic design for my new fliers and my website too!" she exclaimed. "Please call me tomorrow morning so you can help me decide what I need to buy."

Neither woman called the next morning. In fact, they never called.

What's up with that? Aren't they networking to get more clients for their businesses? Here was a client with money who wanted to buy—why wouldn't they call her?

Heidi's experience wasn't the only one. Throughout my networking career, I have heard stories like this over and over again. Once I called a woman who had been a regular at a networking meeting and stopped coming. When I called and asked her why, she said the group didn't work for her—she never got any business from it.

"How many meetings did you go to?" I asked.

"I went to one every month," she replied. (Only one?)

"Did you call people after the meeting?" I inquired.

"No," she said. "If they wanted my services, they would call me." I knew she wouldn't be in business for long.

Here's a tip: *they aren't going to call you.*

Why? Because they have a long to-do list and you're not on it. And a busy calendar, and you're not on that either. You and your products and services are way down at the bottom of their priority list, if you've even made the list. Maybe they haven't done enough comparison shopping yet, or maybe they should remodel the guest bedroom first and wonder if there is enough money for everything. All this thinking starts to become worry, and then it's just easier to forget the whole thing and not talk to you.

And you don't call them, because you don't want to hear all their objections. You want to hear yes but not as much as you are afraid of hearing no.

So most small business owners continue to network and not get the results they want, and they make a lot less money than they deserve. Especially women.

Let's Ask for More Money and Everything Else We Want

There are cultural reasons why women still only make seventy-seven cents to a man's dollar. But some of it is due to our lack of knowledge and skill at negotiating for what we want. Is there a way that we can we take back control of our negotiations, ask for what we want and get it, without being pushy, aggressive, and offending people?

Yes. According to Babcock and Laschever, when women were taught self-management principles, learned to anticipate obstacles that might cause stress and anxiety, made plans to overcome them, set goals for themselves, practiced with a partner to build self-confidence, and rewarded themselves by celebrating the goals they achieved, the gender gap in results was completely eliminated."

In teaching my Financial Stress Reduction workshops, I've seen women—and men too—struggle with pricing. If you don't price your products and services correctly, you won't ever make the money you want—and deserve—to make. Most people have anxiety about asking for money, from negotiating a starting salary to pricing their products and services if they are in business for themselves.

But men were willing to tolerate their anxiety and ask for the money anyway, where women seemed to have much more difficulty with it.

Why are women willing to go broke rather than ask for more money?

Here are some of the responses I've heard as I work with women to improve their financial condition by asking for more money:

- "My clients can't afford more money."
- "Other people are charging less so I have to charge less to be competitive."
- "I'm afraid if I ask for more, I won't get the job (or my clients will leave and I'll have nothing)."
- "I'm afraid if I ask for more, they won't like me."
- "I don't want to be greedy."

And the clincher:

- "I love my work—it's not about the money."

Not caring about the money has cost women plenty.

Some of the reasons why women still don't earn as much as men are listed below:

1. Women don't ask for what they want.
2. They are unsure about what they deserve.
3. They worry that asking for too much might harm a relationship.
4. They fear that people will react badly if they ask for too much.

5. They haven't determined what they want before the negotiation.
6. They ask for their bottom line instead of the top of the line.
7. They often aren't aware of what's possible.
8. They aren't as optimistic as men about their abilities.
9. They compare themselves to other women who are also likely to be underpaid.
10. They expect life to be fair and that they will be offered more money without having to ask.
11. They don't ask for enough or give in too quickly when questioned.
12. They are satisfied with less because they expect less.

The root causes are lack of information, lack of strategies, negative self-image, and fear.

Our society still perpetuates rigid gender-based standards for behavior that require women to behave modestly and unselfishly and to avoid promoting their own self-interest. Women are taught early that pushing on their own behalf is unfeminine, unattractive, and unwelcome—and ineffective because of that.

That's how we are raised and how so many relationship-oriented books teach us we need to be if we are going to have a successful relationship. Although it's estimated that 76 percent of married women work outside the home, they still take the majority of the responsibility for child care and household chores. Women often tell me that their husband "helps them" with the housework. But that still assumes housework is their job, which the men sometimes help with, doesn't it?

In my own family, my sisters both had full-time jobs, yet at major holidays and family gatherings, the women decorated the house, set the table, cooked the dinners, and cleaned up afterward. (I recognize that the men of the family did other chores that contributed, and they're terrific guys!) But everyone seemed to be following stereotypical gender roles when it came to family duties—the same ones we learned from Mom and Dad when we were growing up.

But Mom didn't have a full-time job outside the home. Occasionally, when the topic of dinner table discussion was particularly interesting, I would not get up to help clear the table but sit with the men and continue talking. My sisters never commented on it, but I always felt guilty whenever I didn't get up to help, so I didn't stay seated very often.

When we challenge what feels natural—and it only feels natural because it is what we are accustomed to through habit—we often feel awkward and somehow wrong. But when we continue gender-based role behaviors, we are giving nonverbal instructions to our children about the "right way" to do things.

Linda Babcock told a story about how, even though she made more money than her husband, she let him handle the finances when they went out, pay for dinners, etc. One afternoon, she and her three-year-old daughter went shopping at a drugstore. Her daughter saw a stuffed toy she wanted and asked, "Do you have enough money to buy that for me, Mommy? Do girls have money, or is it just boys that have money?" Linda, of course, was horrified. A simple, seemingly innocuous family habit had communicated to their daughter that men had money but women didn't.

It's all so insidious, and it permeates our daily experience. The National Association of Women Business Owners notes that although women own about 40 percent of all businesses in the United States, they only receive 2.3 percent of the available equity capital needed for growth. Joanna Rees Gallanter, a venture capitalist herself, observed, "Women are often not comfortable talking about what they're worth. They'll go in to pitch a project and naturally put a lower value on it than men do."

The Civil Rights Act of 1964, Title VII, and other legislation made it illegal to discriminate on the basis of gender—overtly. But so much of it is subtle, disguised as socially acceptable behavior, that we don't even see it, or when we do, we think it's just the natural order of things and can't or shouldn't be changed.

In the '70s, I read *Games Mother Never Taught You* by Betty Lehan Harragan. One passage that made a big impression on me was about asking for a raise. She said that most women kept taking on more and more work without asking for more money. Her advice was to "ask for a raise every single time you are told to do anything beyond your original sphere of operation" because "if it's not worth money, it's not worth being done by you." At the time, I thought it was shocking. I also admired the idea and tried to see where I could put it into action. But it felt very scary to me.

I remembered that in my first job after college, I didn't negotiate my starting salary because I was so happy to be offered a job (and I really didn't think I was qualified for it). Then I took on more and more responsibilities until I was doing twice as much work as everyone else in my job category. But when the layoffs came, I was one of those laid off because I was the most recent hire. My employers were very upset at their next business meeting when all the reports I had been doing for them for no extra pay weren't done and they found out how much I had been doing. I wonder what would have happened if I had pointed that out to them beforehand?

The Things You Do Can Cost You, but the Things You Don't Do Can Cost You Everything

Not marketing, not selling, not going to networking events or being active on social media sites, not having a newsletter or writing a blog, and especially not making calls will cost you. As my friend Nancy Sardella, founder and CEO of Worthwhile Referral

Sources, said once at a Women's Referral Sources meeting, "You can't quantify how much business you're not getting through your nonefforts." Brilliant.

The real money you lose in life is the money you fail to earn. How much is that? What if you were able to raise your prices 15 percent but didn't—how much money is that in a year? Five years? What other product or service could you have provided that could have created an additional income stream for your business? What if you had negotiated your starting salary for an additional $5,000 per year twenty years ago? Considering most raises, bonuses, and perks are based on that starting salary, how much have you failed to earn in the last twenty years?

It's adding up to a lot of money quickly, isn't it? But don't despair or spend too much time moaning about the lost income. Instead, look ahead at all the possibilities for creating more income. You want to create multiple streams of income. Invent that new product you've been thinking about. Write a book. Produce and sell a podcast or video. Teach a workshop or a teleclass on a subject you love. License your materials and train others to use them. Start a mastermind group or a networking organization. Sell ads in your newsletters or on your website or blog. Ancillary products can create residual income that continues for years. Raise your prices or ask for a raise. Figure out your value and start earning that now. It's never too late.

What Are the Solutions?

So what can we as women do to improve our experience in the workplace, not only as employees, but also as business owners, freelancers, artists, and salespeople? When we're in charge of creating our own income by getting clients, we have to ask for what we want.

How do we get the courage to do that?

1. Research how much money is available and ask for it.

Studies have shown that gender differences disappear when men and women receive the same information about the going rates for given jobs.

Here's a story I told in my book *The Wealthy Spirit*:

Sally's eyes were snapping and her face burned with resentment. "I've been working for these people for five years and have done wonders for them, but they are so stingy they are only giving me a 3 percent raise!" She was so hot she could barely sit in her chair.

It was a beautiful spring day, and we were sitting outdoors at the local restaurant. I knew something was wrong the minute she arrived. Sally was the executive director of the Chamber of Commerce and was quite visible in the community. She did a wonderful job, and I had seen the growth in membership and programs of the Chamber during her tenure. I had no idea she wasn't well paid.

"Tell me everything," I said, "but start at the beginning. How long have you been working in this job?"

"Five years," she exclaimed, "starting as a part-time secretary. I've been full-time for the past four years and have taken on many more duties and responsibilities. I've tripled their membership and their budget, but they still only give me tiny annual cost-of-living raises based on my starting salary as a secretary!"

She was seething. "I'm going to quit!"

"Take a deep breath and relax a minute," I coached. "You can always quit—that's a last-resort option. But you like the job except for the low pay, so why don't we work together to try to get you the money you deserve?"

She thought about that for a minute, then agreed it couldn't hurt to try.

Over the next couple of weeks, I coached Sally on how to get a raise.

First, I told her to lose the resentment—anger doesn't sell. People just get defensive. Not being well paid was her responsibility and hers alone. She had been waiting for the board of directors to recognize her contributions and voluntarily raise her salary significantly. But she had not given them the facts and figures they needed to justify the increase.

Now she understood, so she put together a presentation for the board that outlined every achievement and the dollar amounts her contributions had made to the bottom line of the organization. She did her research and discovered the pay rates for the same position at similar organizations. She prepared written comparisons of the Chamber budgets for the five years she had been working for them.

We met again at lunch just before her presentation to the board so she could practice her delivery. "You haven't been paying me enough money!" she started out, and I stopped her.

"No resentment, remember? It would have been nice if they had thought that you should be paid more based on the job you have done, but you weren't asking for more, so they thought you were happy. Try it again—be nice, be charming, and be strong at the same time."

She did a masterful job and I told her so. She looked powerful, professional, and determined.

She got a 35 percent raise in salary. We celebrated together that day!

But how much money had she lost for those five years that she hadn't negotiated her salary properly because she didn't find out what she was really worth and ask for it? Think about your own situation—how long have you been underpaid for your talents and skills?

2. Understand that not charging enough is as harmful as charging too much.

Years ago, a friend of mine decided to go into business for herself doing computer consulting. She told me that she had a man who promised to send her a lot of business, so she called him up to tell him she was ready.

"What are you going to charge?" he asked.

"Forty dollars per hour," she replied hesitantly.

"Then I can't send you any business," he stated.

"Why?" she asked. "Is that too much?"

"No," he replied, "it's too little. Any computer consultant worth anything is charging one hundred dollars per hour and up. I can't ruin my reputation by referring people to someone who only charges forty dollars—no one will think you're any good."

You can do yourself irreparable harm if you charge less than market prices. What do you think when people charge too little? I tend to think they are either brand new in their profession or maybe not very good at it—or they don't understand their worth in the marketplace and need some coaching. Arm yourself with good information about the going rates in your profession by checking websites that give information about salary ranges for particular jobs, such as Salary.com, CareerJournal.com, JobStar.org, and Monster.com. Information about salaries in various businesses and public- and private-sector work can be found on websites related to your job-specific industry. Ask your colleagues or anyone you know who uses services like yours. Becoming well-informed about what the market deems work is worth will help you ask for the appropriate amounts and teach you to value yourself and your work accordingly.

3. Research and set an appropriate price.

Get the top figure and the lowest figure. Then pick a price that is in the high middle of that range—studies have shown that to be the most popular price point. They don't want the most expensive because they want to be smart money managers, and they don't want the cheapest because they want to get good value. In the high middle, they figure they're getting good quality at a reasonable price.

When I started my workshops back in 1990, I only charged $200 for the first one. I just made that number up with no evidence or research to support it. I had never taught a workshop before, so I thought I should keep the price low so I could more easily get people to sign up for it. When it was successful, I upped my price the next time—to $350. Then I met a man who taught workshops for $650, and another for $850. So I raised my price to match what I saw others were charging.

Every time I had a price jump to a number that was scary for me, it took me a while to become comfortable saying the new number. I remember having a sales conversation with an insurance broker who wanted to come but wasn't sure it was the right time.

"You'll save money if you register now," I encouraged him. "After the first of the year, I'm raising the price to $1,000."

"Oh, Chellie," he scoffed, "$850 is $1,000. It's not that different."

I thanked him for the tip! And I didn't feel badly about my new price after that. But it didn't roll off my tongue comfortably, so I soon raised the price to $1250 because I could say "twelve fifty" more easily than "a thousand dollars." I made myself another $250 per person just because of that.

Then it was $1595 and then $2000, which again was hard to say, so I went to $2500. Each time I raised my price, I thought I had reached the ceiling of what I could charge, that eventually everyone would say "no, it's not worth it, that's too much." At every price point, some people said it was too much. But at every price point, there were always people who could and would pay.

After that, I looked at the results people were getting from taking my workshop, like the woman who closed a $7 million deal a year and a half afterward, or the financial planner who made $30,000 the first month, or the therapist with ten clients who had twenty-three at the end of the course. Tony Robbins charges $1 million for a year's coaching. There are a number of million-dollar coaches now, with ongoing programs that cost thousands of dollars per month, and a number of them are women. Fabulous! That encourages me that whatever I charge that's less than that is a bargain.

Are you worried about being too greedy if you ask for more? A bad person? Unspiritual? This is often where women get trapped. But just because someone can't afford you doesn't mean you have to price your services to meet their needs. Would you charge five dollars if they could only afford that? There will be other options so they can get what they need—social services, books, tapes, other providers who are less experienced or just starting out who charge less. There is help available at all levels and prices. That's one reason I write books—so I can share some of what I know very inexpensively.

But your time is a finite resource, and for that you need to be paid top dollar. If you were an employee working for a boss, wouldn't you expect to be paid more for your experience than the rookies just starting out?

You're worth more than you think.

4. Ask for the money you want, not what you think you can get.

When you have your own business, you don't have anyone to tell you that you deserve a raise. You have to give yourself a promotion to a new level. Set a goal for yourself of the amount of money you want to earn. Prepare a budget that includes everything you want— the kind of house you want to live in, the car you want to drive, lifestyle you want to live, vacations, travel, and dinners out, and plan adequately for taxes, retirement savings, etc.

A friend of mine told me the story of how she once asked for only $2,500 per month for a salary. It was only later that she discovered that $2,500 didn't even cover her expenses. She said when she realized that she tried to renegotiate, but by then the man who had hired her had lost all respect for her.

One of my clients in my Financial Stress Reduction workshop was a smart, charismatic woman who had also developed an eight-week workshop business helping people with relationships. One evening in around the third or fourth class, she was complaining about how she was unhappy with her income and wanted to make more money. She was charging $400 and wanted to charge $800.

I suggested that, for the next week, she ask for $800 from all her prospective clients. She did and was completely shocked that three people signed up at that price! She couldn't believe it, but I reminded her that I was charging even more than that, and she had paid it.

"Yes," she said, "but you're teaching people about money." I countered that perhaps finding the man of your dreams, having the perfect father for your children, and living with the person you love for the rest of your life was worth a lot too. That shifted her thinking right away.

What comparisons are you making that keep you from charging the money you want?

Every business owner needs to pick two important numbers in their business:

1. How many people do you want to serve each month?
2. How much money do you plan to charge them?

Multiply these two numbers and see if it gives you enough money to pay your bills comfortably, save for the future, pay off your debts, buy a house, go on vacation, and live the life you desire.

If not, you have to pick a higher number!

It sounds simple enough. Just pick a higher number and ask

for it, right? But I know it's hard to get the courage to ask for the money you want alone in a vacuum, with all of society's pressures surrounding you and your old habits of not asking keeping you locked into a financial reality that is less than you deserve.

One thing that will help is to start collecting evidence of other people who are charging what you would like to charge. Look up your competition and see what their prices are. Find some who are charging "outrageous" prices and see how they justify them. Look at your budget—what does it cost you to run your business? To live? To live well? Do you deserve to have nice things? Doesn't it make sense that you charge enough money so that you can have some ease and beauty in your life and vacations too?

Try this exercise: double your current price, write it down, and practice saying it over and over, twenty times a day. Watch how much easier it is to say the number after practicing it for a week than it is at the beginning.

Think about how you would justify your price if someone questioned it. Write down your answers, fine-tune them until you feel you can stand behind them, and memorize them. It might help to get a friend who'd like to make more money and practice with each other until you both sound confident and self-assured about your numbers.

5. Don't reduce your price just because three people in a row say no and you're worried about the competition.

Most people believe the number one factor in buying decisions is price. That's true for some things, but not all.

A woman named Connie wrote me to ask, "What do you do when there are tons of people wanting to undercut the industry?" Her husband was in construction, and after the 2008 real estate debacle, the construction industry plummeted. When jobs were scarce, people started underbidding each other.

This is always the question with a competitive marketplace. Price wars drive down the price for everyone, but there's always a floor that people can't go below or they're working for free. And there are always some talented people who can demand and get higher prices, even in a difficult economy. That's why you work hard to get to the top of your profession and become acknowledged as such.

There's a difference if you're marketing the exact same product, like a coffee mug—if it's exactly the same coffee mug, a consumer wants the cheapest one. But with services, there are other variables. I want the best coach, therapist, chiropractor, doctor, and interior designer I can get, and I understand the best isn't going to be the cheapest. Services take time to deliver and that's a finite resource—you're going to run out of it. If you're selling time, you can charge more the more experienced you are and the more popular you get.

I remember hearing that there are three values in pricing:

1. Good
2. Fast
3. Cheap

A customer can have two of the three but not all three: good and fast but not cheap, good and cheap but not fast, or fast and cheap but not good.

Even with the top-notch professionals, there are people who will bid on their services and ask for deep discounts or "match this bid" or try to tell you the going rate is X and you can't charge more than that, etc. They are welcome to go elsewhere to shop; you don't have to lower your price or your standards. This requires a certain fortitude and determination, as it's scary to turn down work when you've got bills to pay and the next paying client isn't visible.

Are there times when you will lower your price? Sure! Sometimes you've got to make an exception and do the next gig just because you need some dollars in the door today. But if this becomes your habit, you're operating from fear instead of faith. Suddenly, people start to think that you just want X level jobs and start sending those kind of referrals to you instead of the rich, wonderful clients who pay you what you truly deserve. There may be fewer great clients, so you may have to do more marketing and selling to reach them in the numbers you need, but the payoff will be in a richer life.

6. Work for raises more than praises.

During the Great Recession, I watched a lot of people price their products and services so low that they couldn't possibly be making a good living. Some people gave so much away for free that their customers became trained not to pay for anything!

You may want to offer something for free or at a very low price to attract new customers to try out your wares. Many people create a marketing "funnel," where they give away a short report on their website, and then offer a more complete report or an ebook for a small fee. That's followed by an offer for an introductory consultation, which hopefully will result in the customer signing up for a paid service.

You can have many different services at different price points. It's important not to get stuck in the loop of offering too much for free or for low cost. For service-based businesses, I recommend having three packages—bronze, silver, and gold. The bronze package would be the lowest cost and have the least amount of services. The silver would add some additional value, and the gold would be everything you've got.

I recommend against having more than three packages, because too many choices make the customer confused. For your high-ticket clients, you can always add additional services, like a VIP day or weekend at your most exclusive prices.

Free samples are fine, as long as they are samples and hopefully lead into your being able to sell another or similar item or service.

I often do a free one-hour teleclass or speak at a local group for free. That's a great way to advertise if you have a service business. The group already has a mailing list, they have regular attendees at their meetings, they organize and run the meeting, and all you do is speak for half an hour or so and get a free meal to boot.

Besides, I never think I'm speaking for free. I pass out my brochures, have people fill out a rating sheet, call them afterward to thank them for coming, and always sell some books and a workshop or two!

But there's a difference between giving free samples and giving everything away for free. Praises are nice, and some become very valuable testimonials too. But there are limits to how much you can give away and still make a living. At some point, you have to say no to the "it's great PR" opportunity.

It's worth your time to speak for free at a local event that's within easy driving distance. It might not be if you have to get on a plane and spend a whole day traveling. You have to carefully figure out the costs versus the benefits in each case. How many people will you reach? Will you have access to the mailing list? Will you have a table or a booth in the exhibition hall to sell your products and services?

Many organizations and corporations pay their speakers, but not all of them. Years ago when financial author David Bach began speaking, he told speaking coach and author of *Speak and Grow Rich* Dottie Walters that he was going to target women's groups. "Women's groups don't pay," she told him. "Get some sponsors to pay your fees in exchange for advertising." He did that and was very successful.

Women often feel that other women should donate their time and energy for no fee, to help and contribute. There is definitely a time and place for donations of time and energy. But a trade organization, even if it has nonprofit status, isn't the same thing as a charity. You've got to establish boundaries so you do a comfortable level of donating goods and services for free, for great PR, or for praises, but not so much that you aren't earning raises.

I'm looking forward to the day when women's groups make it a priority to hire and pay women really well!

7. Ask for too much!

Doesn't that phrase tickle you? It came up one night in a mastermind group I hold once a month. We were talking about low, medium, and high budgets as we were creating our plans for the New Year. Lynne Azpeitia, an awesome therapist who specializes in working with gifted adults, suggested that we should use our high budget as our low budget instead and then imagine even bigger budgets as our medium and high budgets.

I loved that! Immediately, all of our imaginations caught fire with bigger pictures of what was possible.

Pierre-Augustin Caron de Beaumarchais said, "Where love is concerned, too much isn't even enough." And I thought, why not ask for too much? Too much love, too much money, too much happiness, too much fun.

How often do we restrict our reality to lower levels of possibility by not asking for enough? My friend Carol Allen pointed out to me that it's hard for a massage therapist to charge over $100 because most of them would never spend that amount of money on that kind of luxury item. It's hard to charge $2,500 for a workshop if you can't afford to pay that to attend one.

Alan Cohen, in his book *A Deep Breath of Life*, tells the story of a man who died and went to heaven. God was showing him around, but one door he passed by, saying, "You don't want to go in there." Of course, the man was curious and begged God to let him in. God agreed but told him he would be sorry.

The man gaped at the room filled with amazing treasures and wandered among them until he spied a Rolls-Royce. He ran over to it, saying, "This is the car I always wanted!" Then he saw his own name engraved on the dashboard and asked God why he didn't get this car.

God answered, "Because you asked for an Oldsmobile."

What do you really want? It may already be packaged up, ready and waiting for you. All you have to do is ask for it.

8. Keep going!

Years ago, during one of the first Financial Stress Reduction workshops I ever taught, a woman in my class had a very rich "aha!" experience. Susan was an executive recruiter, bright, fun, and with a sense of ease about her. We were discussing how we worked our businesses, and she mentioned that she just worked until she made a good placement for which she was very well paid and then took time off to play.

"Hmmm," I thought. "She's in my class to make more money. I wonder if she just stops herself when she's made the money she thinks is enough." So I asked her what she thought would happen if she kept going and maybe made another placement instead of stopping at the first one. Her eyes got big and round, and I could tell she hadn't thought of that before.

"I don't know!" she exclaimed.

I said, "This week, keep going and see what happens."

The next week, she announced to the class that she made $35,000 that week! She had no idea she was capable of making that much money.

I thought of this story years later when I was calling people about my next teleclass series. I had a lot of "maybes" on my list—people I had talked to who were thinking it over, wanted to read more about the details of the class on my website, check out the testimonials, check their schedules, etc. I had plenty of people coming. I'm happy and make my budget goals if I get five to six people in each of the three sessions—fifteen people is fine. So usually, I just stop there… but then I remembered Susan's story. What might happen if I just made a few more calls to follow up again with the interested parties who hadn't yet committed?

You guessed it. I enrolled seven more people, for a total of twenty-two. The price of the teleclass was $2,500, so by just pushing myself a little bit, I made an additional $17,500. I can think of some things to do with that extra money too—can't you?

What would happen for you and your budget if you just pushed yourself a little harder at the end of your sales period, so you get that surge of energy that a championship runner feels at the end of the race that pushes him over the finish line first?

Just this week, go for it! And see what happens.

If You Don't Count Your Money, Pretty Soon You Won't Have Any to Count

think I'd better wait until I have more money before I…"

- get an assistant.
- expand my office.
- take a business class.
- hire another employee.
- take a salary for myself.

How long have you been waiting for the extra money to just show up?

Let me give you a tip: more money doesn't appear in your life until you make the commitment to your next level of growth by investing money in it. When you commit time, energy, and money to increasing your income, you take yourself seriously, and others do too.

I'm not talking about going into debt to fund a frivolous trip to the Bahamas or a shopping spree with designer labels you can't afford. That's consumer debt—bad debt.

I'm talking about good debt. Good debt is the money you leverage to make an investment in your business growth and prosperity.

The owner of a $3-million-a-year manufacturing plant told a group of small business owners at the National Association of Women Business Owners (NAWBO) this: "In order to grow your business, you're going to have to get used to bigger and bigger negative numbers."

Gulp. A few sage business owners nodded while everyone else blanched white at that bald statement.

But it's true.

Bill Gates didn't build Microsoft on his personal savings. Stephen Spielberg doesn't finance his own movies.

They use OPM. Other people's money. They borrow money from banks, get loans from friends or family, or get a group of investors to pool their resources to finance growth.

Much of What You Hear from Financial Experts Is Wrong for You

If you're a female business owner suffering from financial stress, I have a message for you: it's not your fault. It's because the standard financial advice you're getting from the usual experts is wrong!

Most of their advice is directed to the large population of worker bees—people on fixed salaries who work at jobs with little potential for growth. But their message is not for *you*.

They tell you to pay off all your debts. Wrong! You will want to get rid of debt eventually, but this should not be your first priority. Steve Jobs got business loans and investors to build Apple. Do you think he spent all his time worrying about how to pay them off? No, and like him, you need to spend your time and energy figuring out how to build your business and make enough money that the debts don't matter.

The Small Business Administration has estimated that it takes one to two years for a new business to become profitable. When Jeff Bezos was marketing Amazon.com, he said that he wasn't trying to be profitable for the first five years. He said he was trying to get users because he knew the profits would follow later—and they did.

Do you think that most entrepreneurs save two years' worth of expenses before they open their business? Certainly not. They have a great idea and convince others to invest in it to help them launch it. Many successful entrepreneurs started their businesses with credit cards and loans from family and friends.

It's important to make a distinction between bad debt and good debt. Bad debt is consumer debt—clothes, restaurants, vacations, cars, etc. It's any money spent on your lifestyle that doesn't enable you to make more money. Good debt is borrowing money to grow your business exponentially so that you have a better product, increase market share, and get more clients.

The experts tell you to stop spending money. Wrong! It takes money to make money. I spoke to a woman who was looking for the cheapest networking group she could attend. She was shocked when I told her she needed to go to the most expensive one. Why? Because the people at the expensive group have money and can afford to pay for your services.

The experts tell you to invest in the stock market. Wrong! The stock market is just group investing in other people's businesses. Shouldn't you be investing in yours?

In September of 2008, as the stock market plummeted and we headed into the Great Recession, I watched in horror as all the talking heads on local and national news channels cautioned Americans to stop spending money: "Pay off your debt, don't buy anything, save your money!" was the standard mantra.

Since 70 percent of the American economy is consumer spending, this wasn't helpful advice. When nobody is buying anything, nobody is selling anything either, which means companies start losing profits, so they cut expenses, stop buying goods and services, and lay off employees.

Of course, if you're an employee, the threat of losing your job and not being able to pay your bills is terrifying. Having the value of your house go down to below the value of the mortgage is just about the worst thing that can happen, because most people's biggest asset is their home and that's what they are relying on to help them retire. So it's not wrong to tell them to save their money and not spend anything they don't need to, because they could lose their income and their assets and be in real trouble.

I think it's much scarier to have a job than to have your own business. When you are employed, all your money comes from one source—your employer. You're like a business owner with only one client. If that client decides to fire you, you have no income at all. But if you're a business owner with fifty clients, some of them may leave, but not all of them at once. You have many sources of income!

It's Never Too Late!

"It's never too late to be what you might have been."

—George Eliot

In the June 2014 issue of *O* magazine, Suze Orman wrote a column about making age-appropriate financial choices. She gave the example of Kimberly, 48, who wanted to leave her corporate job and start a business as a master cake decorator. Although she had eight months of savings set aside to get her business up and running, Suze nixed her idea, saying, "If Kimberly were 22, I'd tell her to follow her dream no matter what. But at 48… No passion project should jeopardize your earning potential in your 40s and 50s—the make-or-break years when you should shore up your retirement savings."

Oh no.

My little corner of the Facebook universe erupted over that.

Mind-set, money, and marketing coach Kate Beeders wrote, "Too old to live your dream?? This advice seems to be coming from a place of fear—not power. This made me so mad. Thank goodness I didn't listen to her!" Others chimed in with "I agree with you. I was 64 when I started my current company," "Wow! If 40-something is too old, I'm in BIG trouble," "Good lordy…I am about to go for my dream…40 is still a babe wet behind the ears, I am starting out again at 74…and I will succeed."

I loved it. There are so many examples of women becoming successful entrepreneurs after forty: Louise Hay started her publishing business Hay House when she was fifty-eight; Mary Kay Ash started Mary Kay Cosmetics when she was forty-five. I started my workshop business when I was forty-two, published my first book when I was fifty-four, my second when I was fifty-eight, and here's my third at the lovely young age of sixty-six. Harry Bernstein, who published his first book at age ninety-six and then three more before passing away at 101, said, "My nineties were the most productive years of my life."

If it wasn't too late for us, it's not too late for you.

What's great about being an entrepreneur is that no matter what the economy and everyone else is doing, you have opportunities to prosper. I teach Financial Stress Reduction workshops, so I knew in an economy that was spiraling downward that I had an unlimited market niche. Of course, so many people were worried about money that it was often harder to convince them to spend money on solving the problem. But I knew that problem would be solved if I just talked to more people.

What's important when the stock market plummets is cash. I suggest you keep a lot of your funds liquid so that when the stock market plummets and the economy tanks (which seems to happen about every eight to ten years), you have money to weather the storm. Yes, I know that you're not making money on that money when it's just held in low-interest savings accounts or CDs. But it's safe, and it feels good to have some money that isn't at risk.

The usual financial experts aren't going to tell you that. They want you to invest your money in the stock market and more risky investments that will earn you a bigger return. They may or may not. It's a gamble. But the experts will certainly earn a bigger commission. So of course they are telling you to save money and invest it. In good times and in bad.

Meanwhile, many small business owners are trying to build their businesses without investing enough money in the things that matter most: sales, marketing, and professional advice such as legal, accounting, intellectual property protections, etc. In *The Millionaire Next Door*, Thomas J. Stanley and William D. Danko say, "The affluent, especially the self-made affluent, are frugal and price-sensitive concerning many consumer products and services. But they are not nearly as price-sensitive when it comes to purchasing investment advice and services, accounting services, tax advice, legal services, medical and dental care for themselves and family members, educational products, and homes."

Retirement

Here's how to calculate the amount of money you'll need at retirement:

Whatever you have now + ten million dollars.

That sounds like enough to make you feel safe, right?

If only all those emails telling me I'd won the Swiss Lotto for $3 million, or I had a long-lost Chinese relative who left me $6.5 million, or a political leader in Nigeria died and his heirs would pay me 20 percent of $10 million were true. I figure I would now have $42 billion. Enough to retire!

I asked several financial advisers I know to estimate the percentage of Americans who can actually save enough money to afford a reasonable lifestyle for twenty-five years without working. Their answer was about 3 percent. In *Pound Foolish: Exposing the Dark Side of the Personal Finance Industry*, Helaine Olen reported that, "Only one in five workers over the age of fifty-five has managed to set aside $250,000 or more for their golden years. These are not exactly sums of money that will go far in retirement, especially when you recognize that many experts in the field believe that people need to save up a minimum of $1 million to get by in their post-work lives, a net worth currently achieved by 8 percent of all households."

You aren't going to save that much by giving up your latte.

Social Security helps—and it isn't going bankrupt, either. Michael Hiltzik's column in the *Los Angeles Times* in March of 2014 outlined the relevant facts: life expectancy has risen since Social Security was instituted in 1935. But the difference is mostly because of improvements in infant mortality. In 1935, if you made it to age sixty-five, you could expect to live to about seventy-seven if you were a man and seventy-eight if you were a woman. In 2009, the figures were eighty-three for men and eighty-five for women. That's an extension of six to seven years, not the decades often reported. And the payroll tax that funds Social Security has increased from 2 percent at its inception to 12.4 percent today.

It will be a thin retirement if that's all you've got, but it certainly helps. If you continue to work part time, have your own business, or start one, you can continue to earn money.

The modern-day concept of retirement has only been around for about seventy years. It was actually designed to get older people out of the workforce to make way for younger, cheaper workers. Before that, work was an inseparable part of life. In the mid-twentieth century, more people had pensions to sustain them when they retired—a guaranteed monthly income that continued until they died. Almost no one has that now, except for government workers.

I spoke with a fiftysomething man who said he was burned out at his job and wanted to retire. But he was afraid. "I have enough money to last twenty years," he said. "But if I live longer than that, it's a problem."

Living too long is a problem? No, the problem is working too hard and burning out. The problem is too much work and not enough vacation. The problem is not having work you love.

I attended an interview with Joan Rivers when she was eighty years old. Asked if she was going to retire, she said, "And do what? No, I love my job," she continued. "I don't want to do anything else." Retirement is for people who hate their jobs. Work is hell when it doesn't match your skills, talents, or interests.

Find work that you love doing and you won't want to retire from it. Retire to do what? How many days do you want to lie on the beach? Ken Dychtwald, PhD, founding president and CEO of Age Wave, a consultancy focused on aging populations, reported that "a lot of people find that they are unhappy and retirement itself is a wasteland. 20 or 30 years of leisure being satisfying is a myth—the average retiree watched 49 hours of television a week last year."

You only think you want to lie on the beach because you haven't had a good vacation. So go to Hawaii or Cabo or the Caribbean or someone's backyard in Malibu now.

And enjoy a latte on the beach while you're at it.

Spend Some Money on Fun Now

"Girls just want to have fun…" goes the Cyndi Lauper song. Boys too, I should imagine. I certainly do.

When it comes to accumulating assets or accumulating

experiences, I fall decidedly on the side of experiences. I want to have fun now; I don't want to slave at a job I hate, waiting for the day I retire to live free and love my life. I was never afraid of dying, but I was very afraid of never having lived. When I read the statistics of how many people die before getting to retirement, I decided to make sure I took plenty of time off to play every year.

You have to figure out what work-life balance you want. Is it okay with you to have less stuff and more memories? Research has shown that at the end of their lives, what most people treasure are their memories of happy times traveling, having adventures, or time spent with loved ones.

I'd much rather travel and remember the wonderful time I had than buy another CD or bond. (I can hear the groan of a thousand financial planners across the land as they read that.) I don't want to buy a house with a big mortgage that I have to pay every month, whether it's a good month in my business or not. With other investments, I can buy more when business is good and less when there's a lull like the Great Recession. (Now the groans come from real estate agents.)

Truthfully, saving and investing is not my area of expertise. I tell everyone they should get some financial planning advice from someone they trust who is an expert. You've got to do something with your excess money (don't you love the sound of that?) after all. Owning a house can be great, and having other investments can be great too. Find a financial adviser or real estate professional who you believe can help you invest wisely while paying attention to your level of comfortable risk.

You just might want to balance it all so that you get some time off and some great vacations too.

I read Dame Judi Dench's autobiography, *And Furthermore*. What a wonderful life she is having! I loved this passage regarding retirement at the end of her book:

You do see people who work toward an age, and then at sixty or sixty-five you see them go into a deep decline, and you wonder: Why? What do you retire for? You retire if you are in a job that has just kept you employed, and given you some kind of income, and then you retire to do things that you really want to do. Well, I am doing the things I want to do now, so I don't want to retire... It is the thing I have always wanted to do, and I am lucky enough to be doing it. You don't need to retire as an actor, there are all those parts you can play lying in bed, or in a wheelchair.

Invest in Your Own Business

People are weird about money.

I've been helping people make and manage money since 1984. Over the years, I've made a study of the inner workings of people's psychology and behavior with money.

For example, people think they're saving money when they don't buy things. Makes sense on the surface, doesn't it? But they tend to not make a distinction between things that are frivolous baubles and things that would help them make more money if they invested in them.

If you're in business for yourself, that idea will get you in trouble. Yes, you need to budget wisely and not overspend. At the same time, you have to invest money in your business before you get a return on the investment. You have to spend money on websites, office supplies, computer hardware, software, training, research and development, trademark protection, insurance, advertising, public relations, etc. Even if it increases your good debt for a time. You have to factor all of that into your pricing to make sure that you are profitable.

You might save money today by not developing a website, but in the long run it will cost you thousands of dollars in lost sales. It's like going to a networking meeting with no business cards or brochure. If you're in business and have all the infrastructure bought and paid for and you aren't getting enough business, you need to invest money in more education—take a workshop or hire a coach or business consultant. You probably need to learn better sales and marketing techniques, and if you don't invest money in that, all the other money you spent on your business is going to go down the drain.

People resist getting additional training because they think if they just work harder, faster, longer, or send out more emails, eventually what they're doing will pay off. But if you're doing the wrong things, doing more of them won't help you at all. Pay the money and get expert help—that's what will save you money, your business, and your sanity.

How to Solve Your Love-Hate Issue with Money

People have funny relationships with money—studies have shown a majority of people believe money is a bad and corrupting influence. But at the same time, they want to have millions of dollars to relieve their fear of financial insecurity! With that kind of ambivalence, it's hard to make money and hold on to it. It's been estimated that about 70 percent of lottery winners are broke within five years. Part of the problem is psychological, and part of it is just plain ignorance of sound money management principles.

Years ago, I read a book on lottery winners and noticed that there seemed to be three things that all the lotto winners did—they bought a new car, took a trip (usually to Hawaii), and they all said the money "wasn't going to change them." Now, if you thought having money was a powerful force for good, wouldn't you say, "Hey, this is really going to change me—I'm going to be a better person now!"?

Rob Anderson of Louisville, Kentucky, purchased a lotto ticket by mistake—he wanted three separate quick picks to give as gifts, but the clerk printed out three quick picks on the same ticket. So he kept that ticket himself and bought three more individual tickets. Guess what? One of the numbers on the ticket he kept due to the mistake won him the Powerball lottery of $128.6 million! When asked what he was going to do with the money, he said he was going to buy a new car and was thinking about taking a trip to Hawaii. (What did I tell you?) But the first thing he said was, "We're really grounded people. My wife taught me well, so to speak, to hang on to that dollar and see how far it gets you. We'll still clip coupons and still look for the clearance rack."

In other words, it "wasn't going to change him." See what I mean?

For all the instant millionaires who go on spending sprees and give away all their money, there are others who save diligently, invest prudently, and never spend a dime.

In November 2013, the *Los Angeles Times* ran an article about an elderly widow who showed up at a small law firm looking for assistance. She needed help managing her estate. When an attorney asked her what she thought she was worth, she said perhaps $40,000. She was quiet and unassuming and had been a first-grade teacher for thirty-five years.

When she passed away in 2011, she left over $5 million to fifteen charities. She had so many assets and papers, it took the law firm two years to unravel it all. The article mentioned she had a Quaker Oats can in a closet that contained savings bonds from the 1940s and 1950s that turned out to be worth $183,000.

We can avoid these two extremes. We can lighten up about money and believe in the good things it can do for us. It can be a powerful force for good just as easily as a bad influence.

Here's how to solve your love-hate issue with money:

1. Make a list of all the things you can do with extra money that will be good for you, your family, your friends, and the world.

2. Say positive money affirmations every day, like, "People love to give me money!", "I am rich and wonderful", and "All my clients praise me and pay me!" They help you stay focused on what you want instead of what you don't want. I believe in this practice so much, I wrote a book filled with them (*The Wealthy Spirit: Daily Affirmations for Financial Stress Reduction*).

3. Write down your million-dollar budget. When you make your million, where will you spend it? Remember that it will probably cost you more money to have a bigger business with more space, employees, advertising, etc. Every dollar you spend is a gift to someone and is enriching others.

4. Design your business plan to generate the money you want. You have to either serve a lot of people for a small price or just a few people for a large price. Which one suits you?

5. Take positive action. You can't wait for your ship to come in if you never send one out. Or, as God said to the man in the story who kept praying to win the lottery, "Buy a ticket!"

You Can't Help the Poor and Starving if You Are the Poor and Starving

I meet so many fabulous entrepreneurs who are so eager to help people and change the world with their wonderful work. But if they don't master how to get paid—and paid well—for their time and energy, they are going to end up broke.

I learned that the hard way myself. When I set out to be a professional actress, I notice I chose "starving actor" rather than "rich famous movie star." It took me many years to figure out that I needed to change my mind-set as well as my actions if I wanted my prosperity to improve.

Women are especially prone to this problem. I think it's because we possess some innate gene or tendency that makes women excellent givers. We need to have that ability to be able to care for children. It's a survival mechanism. It makes us fabulous at customer service, but maybe not so great at sales, earning six-figure paychecks, or promoting ourselves. We have to learn some new tools to be able to do these things if we want to make a good living.

And no, it doesn't mean you have to be pushy, money-grabbing, or arrogant either. That's the real fear behind our reluctance to toot our own horns, isn't it? So we can happily refer people to our friend's business or say others are worth their higher prices, but our client rosters stay thin and filled with people paying discounted rates.

Financial Reports

I hear the wall of resistance going up all over the land.

I know how difficult it is to face the reality of your numbers. Breathe. Relax.

"I don't want to look too closely at my numbers," said a client of mine. "Everything seems to be working out okay and I'm afraid if I look at them too closely, I'll mess things up!" Or as one of my clients said, "I bank at the fog bank."

Here's the truth: your numbers are your numbers. They exist and they are real whether you look at them or not. You're much more likely to mess things up if you don't know what they are.

Can you see the danger that lurks in not knowing? How are you going to make an informed decision about how much to spend on your vacation, birthday party, your daughter's wedding, Christmas presents, or a new car if you don't know exactly how much money is coming in and going out of your bank account?

If you're nervous or scared about your finances and feel out of control with your money, you probably don't have a budget. So start one now. You don't have to buy a fancy program and learn how to install it and use it. Just use a simple Excel spreadsheet. Put columns down the left-hand side and label them income and expenses. Next, put a column on the right for your budget amounts—what you plan to spend on each line item. The third column, to the right of that one, will be what you actually spend.

It may take an hour or so to set it up, but after that, it only takes about two minutes to log your numbers in every time you pay your bills. You'll see what you spent, what bills are still due, how much money has come in, and what's left. This is the greatest management tool ever. Because you won't be able to lie to yourself about your spending anymore.

1. Balance Sheet

When I have people in my classes start adding up their net worth, the tension rises appreciably.

"This isn't reducing my financial stress!" they grumble.

"Not today, maybe," I tell them, "but by the time you finish this class, you're going to be happy you did this exercise. You'll love counting your money when you have more money to count!"

Many people just never get started on the road to financial health because they dread taking a realistic look at where they are now. But until you're willing to look at the sum total of what you are worth, you won't be willing to take action to improve it. And really, hiding out from the truth just puts you under so much tension and stress. You'll always be afraid that you're seriously in trouble with the money game, and that's going to affect everything in your life negatively.

Count it. What if you're better off than you thought and you've been spending all this energy and sleepless nights worrying and fretting for nothing? I've had people come back to class after doing their balance sheet exclaiming that they had no idea they were doing so well—that their net worth was a lot higher than they expected!

I've also had people say their worst suspicions were confirmed. It doesn't matter what the number is today. It's going to change for the better now, because you're taking charge of it. You're going to make new and better decisions about your money, because you're working on it. I know you are because you're reading this book. Good job! Celebrate your richer future—it's on its way because you're taking action now.

2. Income Statement

Otherwise known as the profit and loss statement for business owners, this shows you how much money came in and how much money you spent on tax-deductible business expenses. What is left is either a positive number (your profit) or a negative number (your loss).

Get an accountant or a bookkeeper to prepare this for you with a good computer program like QuickBooks. This is one of those things you should delegate because they can do it faster and better than you while you spend your time doing PR, making more sales, networking, or planning the next phase of your business. "Work on your business, not in your business," as Michael Gerber, author of *The E-Myth*, would say.

I owned a bookkeeping service for twelve years and had thirteen employees. I am perfectly capable of doing my own bookkeeping. But it would be a mistaken use of my energy and talents. If you make $250 per hour, it puts you at a loss to spend an hour of your time doing $50 per hour work. Just because you *can* do it doesn't mean you *should* do it.

Ask your bookkeeper to print your profit/loss statement as a graph. It's amazing what you can learn from seeing the picture of the rise and fall of your fortunes. One of my mentors, Patty DeDominic, asked me to do a graph of the profitability of my bookkeeping service over the prior four years. Even though I knew the numbers, doing it as a graph made certain things stand out.

The graph showed that my business had certain distinct patterns:

I lost money every April and December, and I was most profitable in January, February, June, July, and August. I was able to attack the problems creatively after seeing them so clearly. I overspent on holiday gifts and parties in December, and April was a time extra taxes were due. So I cut back on the holiday spending and found a way to make extra income in April. You might see similar income or spending trends that you can consider when planning your business strategies.

3. Budget (which stands for Baby-U-Deserve-Getting-Every-Thing)

I mentioned low, medium, and high budgets briefly in chapter 2. Here's how to design them. Start with your medium budget first, and write down an estimate of all your income and all your expenses for the month. Make a copy of that budget and cross out whatever expenses you can do without to make your low budget. Finally, think about your financial goals and write down everything you would like to spend money on—a bigger house, new car, bigger contributions to charitable causes, more vacations, etc. That will be your high budget for your rich and successful life.

It may take some time for you to figure these out initially, but after they're done, it will only take you a few minutes each week to log in your income and expenses after you pay your bills and make your bank deposit.

Instructions for Weekly Budgeting Day

1. Have a positive attitude and enjoy counting your money.
   Celebrate and say a prayer of thanksgiving for every dollar of income you received. Congratulate yourself for being a productive member of society and having served your clients really well with products or services you are

proud to have created. Read over some of the glowing testimonials and thank-you notes you've received.

2. Have an attitude of gratitude while you're paying bills.

Say a prayer of blessings as you pay your bills. Say thanks that you have the money to pay for these things, that you are delighted to receive the benefit of whatever the product or service is that you are now paying for. Otherwise, do without it. If you don't like paying the light bill, live in the dark with no phone, no heat, no computer, no Internet. After I told her this, one of my clients exclaimed, "I need a gratitude adjustment!"

I write "Thank you!" on all my checks, although we don't use checks as much now as we once did, do we? But you can write "Thank you!" on your credit card slip too, or just say the blessing as you pay someone with cash. I've been doing this for probably fifteen years or so now.

3. Send the money to others with joy.

Feel the flow of money—it's always moving, coming in and going out. It isn't of any use at all when it's static. It's supposed to be multiplying, and it's supposed to be shared. Every time you pay a bill, you're blessing someone who provided the product or service for you. You are helping them to grow and prosper, feeding their families and maybe their employees too.

So many people get caught up in the fear of lack and limitation with money, afraid to let go of it because maybe they won't get any more. That's just more negative thinking. If you're going to buy the item, be glad to pay for it and enjoy helping enrich another person.

4. Pay something on every bill, or send a note promising a future payment.

I know things get tough sometimes and money gets tight. Maybe you can't pay all that you owe right now and can only make a partial payment. These things happen, and most people will encounter this problem sometime in their lives. The worst thing you can do is stop communicating with your creditors—but that's exactly what most people do.

But if someone owed you money and stopped making payments, didn't send a note, and didn't return your phone calls—what would you like them to do?

If you just send a small check—or a personal note if you truly don't have any money to send—every month, the person to whom you owe the debt will relax and see that you are being ethical and doing the best you can. Call them to arrange better payment terms if you need to.

More money will show up for you tomorrow, because you're doing the work to make it happen today.

Medium Budget

This is your budget for what is actually happening now—your current income and actual expenses.

Business owners often tell me it's too hard to budget because they know what their expenses are, but they don't know what their income is going to be.

Here's how to figure what it has to be:

> **Total Personal Expenses + Total Business Expenses =**
> **Total Income Required**
>
> **Do the math.** How many people do you need to serve at what price to make the money you want? If you need to make $8,000

per month, you can have eight clients at $1,000 or sixteen clients at $500, or sell 8,000 $1 items or 1,000 $8 items.

The formula is:

Yearly Income / Number of Clients (or Products) = Price

Or you can do it this way:

Yearly Income / Price = Number of Clients

Let me be clear: your income may fluctuate from month to month, but you have at least an approximation of what your income is going to be. What do you do to produce income, and can you do more of that to ensure that you make enough? What additional sources of income can you rely on?

For budgeting purposes, if you've been in business for a while and have a track record, take your total income for last year, divide it by twelve, and you'll have your estimated monthly income. If you're just starting out, you'll have to guess, but pick a number and then do everything you can to make that number happen. When you commit to your numbers, you'll be amazed at the creative ideas you have to honor your financial commitment to yourself.

Low Budget

This is the tighten-your-belt budget—the one everyone's afraid they are going to have to be on if they look too closely at their finances. My friend Carol Allen calls this the "Oh Shit Zone."

But if you don't face it up front, you're never going to have the clarity to know how to get out of low budget and into medium or high budget.

A journalist I know wrote me to ask what I would say to a sad reader of hers who was disabled at fifty-seven and in credit card debt. She gets a small monthly disability check and has a house paid for, but nothing else. Did I have any words of wisdom for her?

Yes. People do get themselves into some pickles, don't they? I know they want a magic answer to have their debt disappear, but it's going to take money, which means it's going to take work.

I know life gets tough sometimes. It's hard to keep believing that things will get better when the economy is in trouble and nothing seems to point to a better day. There is a better day coming, but you have to take the right steps to make sure you're in the sunlight when that day arrives. There is no magic answer. You have to find some work you can do to bring in money—either employment in a job or start your own business.

I met a woman once who owned a very successful employment agency. When I asked her how she got started, she said she was in a serious car accident and was hospitalized for almost a year. She was her own sole support, and she said she had to find a way to make a living from her hospital bed. Immobilized, she couldn't move anything but her mouth, so she said to herself, "Well, I can talk on the phone so I'll do telephone sales." And that's how she started her business.

What talents or skills do you have that people might pay you for? Look in the want ads, post your résumé online, and talk to friends or old employers. You could start your own business on a shoestring if it's service-based, but eventually it's going to require more money.

The only thing that will keep you going is your strength of will. You determine what you want to happen and you dedicate yourself to doing whatever it takes to make that happen.

Educate yourself. You may need to upgrade your skills, take classes, read books, listen to podcasts, or watch videos. There's an abundance of information on the Internet. Get a mentor or find someone to partner with you who has different skills than you do. Join or start a mastermind group of friends who can help and support you and each other. You can do your own self-study program.

Even if you have a long-range plan to save for a down payment on a house or dig yourself out of debt, it will be too depressing if you think about living on the cheap for too long. Try to be cheerful during your low budget days and know that they aren't going to last forever. Something great could happen today or tomorrow or next week, and you could move up to medium budget! Then you're going to do your positive affirmations with more energy and excitement, and that will have big payoffs in your daily joy and prosperity.

Whatever budget you're on, always make sure you are living below your means. Committing to too many ongoing monthly expenses without leaving room for savings, emergencies, or opportunities isn't going to make you a happy camper when the economy tanks, your child needs an operation, or the family breadwinner loses their job. This past recession has taught that lesson, but has everyone harkened to it? Or will the spending splurge start again immediately?

Bankruptcy

Sports Illustrated says 78 percent of NFL players go bankrupt or are under financial stress within two years of retirement.

That's a shocking number. It surprised me when I discovered how many famous, successful people have filed for bankruptcy. I had to file for bankruptcy myself in the early '90s. I lost a major client and got stuck with a 16 percent underwater mortgage when a housing bubble collapsed. (For the whole story, see my book *Zero to Zillionaire*.) I took comfort from the fact that I wasn't alone. Life is risky and you don't always win, but you can always recover.

Mary Pickford, the silent film star, said a beautiful thing that comforted me when times were tough: "If you have made mistakes, even serious ones, there is always another chance for you. What we call failure is not the falling down, but the staying down."

Now is the time to plan a better future. While you do that, figure out some low-cost pleasures that are really fun. Pack a picnic lunch and go to the beach, lake, or park. Spend a day at a local art or natural history museum. Pop some popcorn and rent a movie. Invite your friends over for a potluck dinner. Some of the best times I've had in my life were with friends when we were on low budget.

Here are a few notable people who filed for bankruptcy but won their way back to a rich and wonderful life:

Kim Basinger	Barry Manilow
Toni Braxton	Willie Nelson
Nicolas Cage	Wayne Newton
Francis Ford Coppola	Randy Quaid
Walt Disney	Scottie Pippin
Henry Ford	Dave Ramsey
Dorothy Hamill	Lynn Redgrave
Mark Victor Hansen	Burt Reynolds
Milton Hershey (founder of	Mickey Rooney
Hershey's, filed four times)	Charles Schwab
Conrad Hilton	Mark Twain
Thomas Jefferson	Mike Tyson
Jerry Lewis	Sam Walton
Abraham Lincoln	

High Budget

This is the success budget—the rich one you get to live on when your business soars and you start making all the money you want! Why do you want more money? What are you going to spend it on?

Barbara Barschak, a partner at the Katz Cassidy accounting firm, told me that one of the pleasures for her of being on high budget is that she doesn't have to stay in "thin hotels" any more. When I asked her what she meant by that term, she said, "Everything is thin in them: thin sheets, thin towels, thin walls, thin carpet, thin drapes."

The first time I made a high budget for myself, it became my medium budget within four months. That's the power that comes from giving yourself a goal and then motivating yourself to get it. A high budget is a positive affirmation of your success in numerical form.

You have to master the numbers. Not only to create the money you want, but also to conserve and protect the money once you get it.

Several years ago, Oprah had a homeless man on her show along with two documentary film producers. The producers had placed a briefcase filled with $100,000 cash in a Dumpster and waited for this homeless man to find it. They were doing a study to see how he would respond and if the money would change his life.

They offered him a financial adviser to help him set up a budget and teach him how to manage it, but he didn't take them up on it. He got an apartment, furniture, television, car, and a girlfriend. He gave a lot of the money away to friends. He blew through all the money in about six months.

The money in the suitcase looked like untold riches when he had nothing. But when he upgraded his lifestyle, it ate up the money quickly. Before he knew it, the money was gone and he was back on the streets.

You, however, are a smart money manager, always keep track of your income and expenses, and have savings and a "rainy day" fund. Then you get to have some money to play with, but not so much that you end up with nothing.

Nancy Sardella gave this instruction in one of her marketing seminars: "Stop clipping coupons and spend that extra hour on your marketing plan!"

Getting smaller won't help you go big. Design your high budget and look at it every day. Put your creative brain to work: revise your marketing plan, make another sales call, write an article, post on your blog, post on Facebook, write an interesting tweet, get together with a friend and brainstorm ideas, raise your prices, or add a product or service.

Living within your means is important, but not as important as increasing your means. Go make better means today!

Spree Budget

I love feeling responsible. It makes me feel like I am a good citizen, a proper role model, smart, savvy, and together. I'm taking care of the future, storing my nuts for the winter like the squirrels in my backyard. Having some money in savings makes me feel safer.

But then I can get bored and need to spice up my life a bit. At those times, I love throwing caution to the wind, escaping the bonds of frugality, and splurging on fun, excitement, travel, and fine dining!

I used to think the critters in my backyard never did that because they all seemed devoted to searching for food, building a nest, and attracting a mate. But sometimes, the birds just sit in the trees and sing, apparently for no reason except to revel in the sound of their song. I think the life lesson of that is: when you've had some success, be sure to take some time off to sing!

Sometimes we get so caught up in our obligatory bills that we forget that we need to nurture ourselves by spending money on something fun once in a while.

It doesn't have to be a big sum or a big purchase. It can be a little thing like an ice-cream cone in the middle of the day, going out to your favorite restaurant for dinner, buying that pretty necklace that makes you feel like a million bucks, or taking a morning off and springing for a round of golf. (If it's on a work day, you will have the added pleasure of playing hooky.)

Don't let any negative self-talk get in the way of your delight. Your job is to fully experience and relish enjoyment and pleasure!

This is a gift you give yourself. You work hard, you show up for your family and friends, you have problems that you face and challenges you overcome. You get to relax and have fun too.

But what about the future?

My mother didn't work outside the home, so she didn't officially retire, but she died at age sixty-seven. That seems so young to me. (And it seems younger and younger every year as I age.)

I'm sure glad she didn't wait until retirement age to have a good time. She and Dad and our family went out to dinner, put on parties, had weekend getaways with friends and summer weeks at the beach, vacationed across the country to visit relatives, traveled, and played golf.

Every day in the news, I see people who have passed from this life, some early, some late. None of us knows the time of our passing, only that it will come. When told life is a journey, not a destination, I've heard it said that "You'd better enjoy the journey—the destination of life is death." Yowza. I never thought of it quite like that, but it's true, isn't it?

So live a little and give a little. Buy the candy or the Girl Scout cookies from the kid who comes to the door. I have a rule that if a child comes to the door selling something, I buy it. I want to give them a happy sale in remembrance of all those nice people who said yes to me when I was the nervous kid at the door, hoping for a sale.

No, we can't splurge and spend all our cash the minute we get it. We want to have some money and resources saved in case we make it to "Super Senior" status, as my dad used to call the stage of life after eighty-five. But I see too much money in the bank as just a lot of wasted opportunity.

One of my favorite splurges happened in Rome with my good friends, Shelley and Bobbi. We saw this beautiful shop filled with delicious ice cream. Customers piled their ice-cream cones high with various luscious flavors and then topped them off with flags, Eiffel Towers, curlicues, etc. We had never seen cones so ornately decorated. Like schoolgirls, we were enamored and kept piling things on.

We had no idea how much we had spent until we went to the checkout counter. Each cone was twenty-five dollars! We were so shocked! But you can't return an ice-cream cone, so we just giggled and ate them up. Our friends back home had a good laugh when I said our trip was on the "Shelley Lavender see-Europe-on-$2,000-a-day plan."

So today, go splurge a little with my blessings!

Debt and Credit Cards

There weren't any credit cards back in the '40s and '50s when my parents were just starting out and raising their family. Most people would get a mortgage for their house and a bank loan for their car, but that was about it. It was all cash all the time after that.

There were limitations to that financial reality, but perhaps easy credit hasn't been so easy on us. Endless streams of advertising on television, newspapers, social media, and every website tell us we can have our dream for only $99 down and $49 a month. We've got the $99 and we'll figure out a way to get the $49 later.

You see the problem. It works as long as everything goes perfectly, but what's the plan if you get sick, or lose your job, or your kid needs braces, or fill in the blank? We want to be optimistic, but we also want to guard against possible losses.

I love credit cards—they are wonderful for keeping track of monthly expenses, tax-deductible receipts, and for borrowing money when it's a judiciously deliberated decision. Many a small entrepreneur got their start through a credit card loan.

But sometimes you can just save the money and buy the thing you want after you've got the money. Don't forget that's an option.

Maybe you don't pay by check as often as you once did, instead paying bills through online banking, automatic charges to your bank account, or using credit cards. It's still important to keep track of your spending, no matter what method of payment you use. How many of you are surprised when the credit card bill comes in to see how much money you spent? Credit cards are handy tools, but you get in trouble when you don't keep track of how much money you actually have.

There was a time when credit cards weren't accepted at the grocery store (until they discovered that people spend between 30 and 40 percent more if they can charge it). I went to the store with a certain amount of cash, and if my total went over that amount at the cash register, I put things back. Now my tendency with the credit card is to just buy whatever I want and worry about paying the bill when it comes in next month. I have a pretty good feel for my ballpark figure of food expenditures, but sometimes it goes a bit over what I expected, and I think back—did I really need to buy the garlic butter spread? I only used it once…

What helps this situation is to have a check register for credit card charges. Write them all down as they occur, just like you do with checks. Then you'll never be surprised at your bill again, and it just might stop you from spending on unnecessary items.

What do you do to keep your credit card charges in line with your budget?

How to Pay Off Credit Cards

1. List all the credit cards with an outstanding balance in order of interest rate, the highest one first. That's the one you want to pay off first.
2. If you have one or two credit cards that have balances that

are much smaller than the others, move them to the top of the list. You'll pay them off first and feel successful that you accomplished this goal, and that helps spur you on to pay off the next one.

3. Pay more money to the first one on the list—I suggest double whatever you're paying on the others. This will accelerate that one getting paid off and you'll see it happening faster. Focus on the good feeling you get as you see your balance going down each month.

4. Continue to write "Thank you" on every check.

5. Stop thinking badly of yourself for being in debt. You're a smart money manager who borrowed some money once and is responsible and paying it back now.

6. Only think about debts on bill-paying day. Every other day, focus on how to make more money!

7. Celebrate every time you finish paying your bills—give yourself a reward for being a good money manager! (A little reward—not something you use a credit card to buy.)

Savings and Investments

"Pay yourself first!" is the lesson of *The Richest Man in Babylon*, a great little fable written in 1926 by George Clason. Or, as one of the participants in my workshop said, "Savings accounts are for saving, and I need to be saved!"

Years ago an actor friend of mine, Joey, got a regular part in a TV series. He told me all the other guys in the cast went on a spending spree, splurging on cars, houses, fine wines, fancy watches, vacations, etc. Joey put all his money in savings. "That's my insurance policy that I'm never going to have to be a waiter again," he said.

Our economy cycles through seasons of lack and seasons of plenty. I remember the recessions in the early '70s, '80s, '90s, and

2000s. These downturns were always followed by upturns and the economy soared once again.

Somehow, during times of plenty, it feels like the good times have come to stay: we made it through the storm, survived, and now we're doing great again and we've finally got it! We're successful and we're going to be on top forever! Or so we think.

That's why people start charging up their credit cards again—they've been on low budget and now there's more money, and they want to splurge on high budget. They're free to do some of the things they couldn't do when money was tight.

That's fine. You should have some spree money when the economy loosens up. But you've got to carefully figure out how much and for how long. Otherwise you get caught up in a new habit of spending and forget to store up your grain for the lean years.

Do not mistake it—lean years will come again. Have fun, enjoy your money, and have the good life. Just make sure to have some cash reserves too.

Note: a zero balance on your credit card doesn't count as a reserve.

The Twelve-Step Program for Financial Stressaholics

With a wink and a nod to Alcoholics Anonymous and twelve-step programs everywhere, here are the twelve steps to treat your money disorders—spending bulimia and income anorexia:

1. We admitted we were powerless over money—that our checkbooks had become unmanageable.
2. We came to believe that a budget greater than ourselves could restore us to sanity.
3. We made a decision to turn our will, insurance, checkbooks, and retirement accounts over to the care of a financial adviser that we understood.

4. We made a searching and fearless moral inventory of our debits and credits.
5. We admitted to God, to ourselves, and to another human being the exact nature of our accounting errors.
6. We were entirely ready to have our financial adviser remove all these defects of our accounting software.
7. We humbly asked her to adjust our bank reconciliations.
8. We made a list of all persons to whom we owed money and became willing to pay them all.
9. We made direct payments to such people wherever possible, except when to do so would overdraw our bank accounts.
10. We continued to take financial seminars, and when we were wrong promptly admitted it.
11. We sought through prayer and meditation to improve our conscious contact with our financial adviser, praying only for knowledge of her retirement plan for us and the power to invest enough money in it.
12. Having had a spiritual awakening as the result of these steps, we tried to carry this message to income anorexics and spending bulimics and to practice these principles in all our finances.

Live long and prosper!

Selling Is Serving—Somebody Needs Your Help!

"I don't care how many degrees you have on the wall, if you don't know how to sell, you're probably going to starve."

—George Foreman

Everything has to be sold—every service and every product. If you want a job, you have to sell an employer on hiring you. Once hired, you'd better keep selling them on how well you're doing too. Your company exists to sell something, and the more you know about sales, the more valuable an asset you will be to them. If you want to climb the corporate ladder, it's usually located in the sales department.

If you own a business, you have to find a steady stream of customers who want what you have and keep them coming back for more. Perfecting your skills in your profession or gathering more credentials won't help you if you can't sell.

The first step in sales is marketing. The second step is selling. You need both steps, and they are completely different. Don't confuse the two. And don't leave either step out.

The distinction is this: marketing is getting the word out, and sales is getting the money in. Many women have trouble with one or both of these steps, largely because they fall under the category of "tooting your own horn." And that makes women uncomfortable, because we don't want to be seen as arrogant or boastful, cocky or brazen. Society reinforces the idea that women who are too forward are unfeminine, and both men and women harbor these opinions.

But every dollar in your bank account is a testimonial from the people you helped. You believe your product or service really helps people, don't you? Don't lots of people thank you for it? Aren't they richer, happier, prettier, healthier, less tired, more productive, or otherwise better off because of it? Then it stands to reason that if you withhold it from people by not promoting it and talking about it, then you are doing them a *disservice*!

Another reason we don't make sales calls is because we're not good at it. Who likes to do things they're not good at? It's much less threatening to write another blog post than call someone. It's much easier to post something on Facebook than to suggest you find a time to talk with one of your Facebook friends and get to know them better.

It takes time and study to learn new skills, and you may not be good at them immediately. But I've seen a lot of people claim they aren't good at calling people after only a few tries. If you were taking piano lessons, you wouldn't expect to be playing beautiful music immediately. You'd be aware there was a learning curve and be willing to spend some time, energy, and money on learning how to play. You'd give yourself a break when you made mistakes and keep trying until you got it right. Then you'd take the next lesson or pick up the next piece of music and practice it until you got it right. You wouldn't think you were stupid or bad or wrong if you didn't do it perfectly right out of the gate!

But of course, you practice the piano alone at home, right? Practicing marketing and sales is visible to lots of people! That's plenty scary. But you know what? These are risks you have to take if you want to get your work out into the world. There are always going to be more people.

If you just keep practicing, you'll get better at it. And then you'll be successful and you'll help a lot of people. And that will be worth it.

Instead of "Selling," Call It "Convincing" or "Persuading"

Back in my previous lifetime when I was an actress, I had to put myself outside my comfort zone all the time at auditions. Actors probably spend more time on job interviews than they do working. Someone said to me once that all my experience in the acting profession must have helped me get used to rejection. Oh, yeah. You never like it, mind you, but you get over thinking that the world will end because one audition went badly, or they liked you but they wanted a tall blond instead of a short redhead…

One audition I went on was for models for the Los Angeles Auto Show. You know, the tall beautiful spokesmodels in the gorgeous gowns who stand next to the cars and talk about them? Well, this wasn't exactly my type, but I went to the casting call anyway because I needed some work.

This job was for Oldsmobile, and I decided I was just going to charm the man running the show into hiring me. So I kept smiling and joking and being personable as he rejected girls, saying "thank you for coming," and kept a smaller pool of us to the side.

Finally, there were about five of us left. The other girls were all so tall! (I'm 5'4".) He gave the four other girls the hiring forms and asked me to come into his office. He said, "I'm not sure what to do with you. You're not really the type we usually hire for this job."

"I know," I said. "I knew that when I showed up today. But I have a different take on what this job is all about. If you hire me, I'll sell cars!"

He laughed, shook his head, grinned at me, and said, "Okay, you've got a job!"

He gave me the hiring forms, and I said, "I need the information on the cars you're going to have at the show." He was surprised but gathered up a bunch of brochures for me to take home.

I studied them and memorized the stats. On the weekend of the show, I stood by the cars, smiling and greeting everyone who passed by. When someone looked interested, I'd lift up the hood and explain about the engine. I'd sit them in the driver's seat and have them feel the luxurious leather and notice the rich interior. I made them feel good sitting in it. A lot of them asked about purchasing, so then I'd send them over to the guy who hired me. He was so happy!

At the end of the auto show, he offered me a full-time job working for him selling cars. That still tickles me.

To get the gig at the Auto Show, I first had to sell this man on hiring me. I didn't think of it as selling then. I just thought of it as convincing him to give me a chance. Convincing, persuading, selling—it's all the same. As a woman, you are a natural persuader. You convince your kids to pick up their rooms, do their homework, get good grades. You persuade your husband or partner to take you out to dinner or go with you to the movie you want to see. You're talking people into things all the time! Convincing someone to try your product or service is the same thing.

The Importance of Promotion

I started writing my first book, *The Wealthy Spirit*, in 1998. At that time, I didn't know anything about the publishing industry. I just knew I had some information to share that I thought would help people. So I bought *How to Get Happily Published* by Judith

Appelbaum and *The Shortest Distance Between You and a Published Book* by Susan Page and signed up for Mark Victor Hansen and Jack Canfield's seminar "How to Build Your Speaking and Writing Empire."

I'll never forget the moment Jack turned to the audience and said, "After you've written your book, found an agent, gotten a publisher, and your book is finally in the bookstores, five percent of your work has been done."

Yikes.

You learn that, in the book world, PR is everything. When you walk into a bookstore, you are walking into a treasure house of several hundred thousand books. Online at Amazon.com, BarnesandNoble .com, and others, you can find millions of books. According to *Publishers Weekly*, in 2010, there were 316,480 new print titles issued by U.S. publishers and more than 2.7 million "nontraditional" titles were also published, including self-published books, reprints of public domain works, and other print-on-demand books.

Somewhere in your mind, dimly, you knew that, but nothing drives it home so much as walking into a bookstore and seeing rack upon rack of beautiful books. Then you go find your section and see all the racks of beautiful self-help books. Then, tucked into a small shelf on the bottom left, there is your one and only, your own beautiful book. *Ahhh*, you sigh. Your book, your dream, has magically materialized and actually exists in a real bookstore in real space in real time. Then your eyes widen, you look around, and you think, "Gadzooks (or some such expletive)! How am I going to get my book noticed?"

The answer is PR, PR, PR, and more PR. As in public relations, press, advertising, newsletters, e-zines, magazine articles, newspaper articles, radio if you're lucky, television if you're really lucky, and then there's all the social media too. You put on your gold tennis shoes and do a book signing, speak at the Lions Club, the Direct Marketing

Association, the Church of Religious Science, the Women's City Club, the Society for Technical Communication, and anywhere else that will book you. You go to other people's book signings and schmooze, give copies of your book to celebrities (Marianne Williamson, Mark Victor Hansen, Martha Beck, and Suze Orman all own personally autographed copies of *The Wealthy Spirit*). You go to your six or seven regular networking meetings, National Association of Women Business Owners, Women's Referral Service, Chambers of Commerce, Le Tip, etc. (It really helps if you like chicken.)

You do all this because, when you have lunch with Michelle Anton, the producer of the *Dr. Laura* radio show, she tells you how she found out about your book—that she didn't know that you were on the *Dr. Laura* television show three years earlier, she didn't get the press release your publisher sent with your book, and she didn't get your letter that you sent with your book.

None of that mattered. What mattered was that a friend of hers told her about the book. And that's why when someone asks what marketing strategy has worked the best to promote your book, you say, "The twenty years I've been out there networking."

Then, because book money comes three months after the end of the six-month royalty period, you make hundreds of gold calls on the gold phone because you have to enroll people in your workshops *now* so you can live until the *later* money of books comes in the mail. You teach class two nights a week and enroll class every other day. In your spare time, you blog, write an article for another website, write your next newsletter, and smile sweetly when people start asking you about your *next book*…

And you thank God every day for giving you this rich, full, high-class-quality-problem, too-busy life where you can decide what dream you want, bring a book into being, and e-zoom your thoughts, advice, strategies, and feelings into the minds and hearts of a circle of people who become your friends and colleagues.

If you've ever written a book or want to, taken on a big project at work, or started your own business from scratch, you know the time and dedication it takes to bring it to fruition. The good news is that if you're successful, marketing and sales never ends. The bad news is that if you're successful or not, it never ends.

When I started writing *The Wealthy Spirit*, I gathered four other writers and started a mastermind group. Linda Sivertsen was the only one who had a traditionally published book at that point—the rest of us were madly writing, looking for agents, publishers, etc. As my publication date approached, Linda gave me a piece of advice I never forgot: "When your book comes out, so much is going to come at you, it will make you crazy. You can't possibly do it all. You'll say yes to some things you should have said no to, and no to some things you should have said yes to. You just have to do the best you can and then go to sleep at night."

I think that's useful for all of us all the time. I'm single and have no children, so I have more time to devote to writing, marketing, speaking, publicity, and all other business tasks. If you have a family with small children, a lot of your time is necessarily going to be invested in them, as in any big project you might undertake. It doesn't mean you can't be successful—it just means you're going to have less time right now. Nobel Prize winner Toni Morrison started writing when she was raising two children and teaching at Howard. She said she wrote "at the edges of the day," before the kids got up in the morning and after they went to bed at night.

The Most Common Problem—Shipping

If there's a problem in the business, the problem is usually in the shipping. Not the postal service, FedEx, or UPS shipping, but what I call "sending out ships"—sales calls, marketing, advertising, anything you do to get customers or clients. I took this analogy from the merchants in London in the 1800s who sent out ships to trade in foreign ports for various consumer goods. Once the ships were launched, it could take some time for them to return, but when they did, the merchants' fortunes were made. And that's where the expression "waiting for my ship to come in" came from.

But you can't wait for your ship to come in if you don't send any out! So I call all my marketing and sales activities "ships" that I send out so that one day they can sail back into my harbor loaded with treasures. It's also more fun and less challenging to "send out twenty ships" today instead of "make twenty sales calls."

Here are some samples of ships you can send out:

- Ads online—on websites, social media, Google, etc.
- Ads in newspapers and magazines—the ones your customers read
- Ads on television and radio—national spots can be very expensive, but local venues less so
- Apps for smart phones—what can you invent that lots of people would use?
- Listings in membership directories—local or national, print or Internet
- Networking—make your thirty-second introduction your commercial
- Speeches—give paid keynotes, or free spots for exposure to your target audience
- Facebook—contribute to conversations and call some of your friends
- LinkedIn—post your information, join or create interest groups
- Twitter—tweet regularly, follow others in your field
- Google+—don't just advertise, socialize
- Pinterest—pin photos with quotes that relate to your business

- Other social media and membership groups
- Newsletters—gather an email list of customers and prospects and send them articles
- Blogs—publish your own and guest post and comment on others
- White papers—write in-depth, well-researched articles about a subject
- Press releases—get the word out about what's new or entertaining about you or your business
- Joint ventures—get together with some colleagues to put on a conference or telesummit
- Affiliate programs—pay a referral fee to people who send out your information to their lists
- Conferences—good places to network and to speak
- Website—offer free reports, videos, or podcasts so people sign up for your mailing list
- Membership site—charge a monthly or yearly fee and offer benefits
- Squeeze page or sales page—a landing page apart from your website with a special offer
- Shopping cart—install a program so people can buy your products directly online
- Books and ebooks—*The Wealthy Spirit* was the best brochure for my workshop I ever created
- Book signings—people like to meet authors and hear them talk about their subject
- Free teleclasses—build your list and give prospective clients a sample of your work
- Free consultations—offer the first meeting at no charge
- Free samples—give away a sample of your product or a recording of a talk
- Advertising specialties—pens, T-shirts, coffee mugs, etc.

- Videos on YouTube—your video could go viral or you could have your own channel
- Fliers—have handouts when you speak
- Podcasts—record a speech and list it on iTunes
- Postcards—local businesses can send coupons for discounts or advertise an open house
- Word of mouth—ask customers who they know who might like your services too

What else do you do and what works best for you to bring in business?

A zillion years ago, back in the Dark Ages before the Internet, I started my workshop business. At the time, Tony Robbins had an infomercial running every night on cable TV. Well, I knew I wasn't going to be doing that anytime soon, so I decided I would do my own version of an infomercial live at networking groups where I would give my thirty-second commercial. Then I booked speeches at various local groups in Los Angeles. I invited people to my office in the evenings for a free seminar. I mailed out brochures and fliers. I ran ads in the local papers.

All this was a lot less expensive than an infomercial.

Some women tell me they're terrible at networking. That's like saying you're terrible at parties, or at church, or on a committee. Most women I know are naturally caring and want to be helpful. So use that—go to the group with the mind-set that you're there to be helpful to others. Act like you're the hostess of the meeting and be there to greet others and make *them* feel comfortable. Volunteer for the welcome committee where it will be your job to do that.

The biggest mistake I see people make at meetings is they try to pitch themselves all the time. They join a group conversation and quickly try to turn the conversation to their business instead of asking other people about theirs. (Note: men are particularly egregious at this. Guys, women really like it if you act interested in them rather than brag about yourself.) If everyone in the group does that, not many referrals are going to result because everyone's focus is on themselves. But if everyone tries to find referrals for the other people in the group, many more referrals will result.

Nancy Sardella began Women's Referral Service (and added Worthwhile Referral Sources because so many men joined it) in 1977 because she couldn't find a referral to a female doctor. She set up the group from a feminine energy model. At their meetings, you're taught the best way to network: introduce yourself and immediately ask the other person what they do and what kind of clients they're looking for. It's much friendlier than walking up to a stranger and saying, "Hi, let me tell you about me, my wonderful service, and why you should buy it."

Where to Network

You want to find networking groups that are filled with upbeat, friendly people. If you sell products to large corporations, you want to attend groups where the corporate buyers are. If you provide personal services like makeup, you want to attend meetings at women's groups.

You can start with your local Chamber of Commerce, National Association of Women Business Owners, eWomenNetwork, or any group you've heard of. You can google "networking" and the name of your city and see what comes up at a time and place you can get to.

Go to a meeting with the idea that you want to meet as many great people as you can. Go up to the first friendly face you see and introduce yourself. You can say something like, "Hi, I'm new here. Have you been a member long?" That should start the conversation rolling—if they're a member, you can ask them to tell you about the group, and then ask about their business and get their card. If they're also new, they'll be delighted that they have found another new person to talk to.

To find a group that's looking for a speaker, google "networking," "speaker," and the name of your city. You'll find a number of groups that have speakers, so you can go to their websites and find out who to contact. Rotary Clubs are great places to start practicing speaking. They meet every week and have a speaker for twenty-five minutes. The program chair has to book fifty-two people during the year, so you can bet they are going to be glad to hear from you!

Let me give you a tip: the most important time of a networking meeting is *after* the meeting. After you've given your thirty-second commercial or your speech and the meeting is adjourned, people have a chance to come over to you, introduce themselves, and talk to you about your business. It's amazing to me how many people jump out of their chairs and run to the parking lot as soon as the meeting is over. Maybe they're late to their next appointment, but I say don't schedule any appointments for an hour after the meeting is over so you can linger and chat with the people you met. Everyone there is a potential customer, could refer a customer, or could be a strategic alliance for you. Some of them will want to use your services. You'll want to use some of their services.

If I'm a regular member of a group, I always make it a point to greet newcomers and make sure they feel welcome and want to come back. One rainy morning after a networking brunch, I gave a ride home to a new member who had just moved to Los Angeles from out of state and had taken the bus to get there. We got to have a lovely chat on the way home. Maybe she'll be interested in my workshop one day or know someone who will. Maybe we'll become friends or colleagues. Or maybe I just got to do a good deed and feel good about it. Who knows? But possibilities become opportunities in moments like this.

Give yourself time for making friends and doing good deeds at the end of meetings.

Following Up with Your Contacts

Laura Arnold is a fabulous relationship therapist in Los Angeles. I met her through the Worthwhile Referral Sources (WRS) networking group. Recently, we were both asked to give a testimonial on behalf of WRS at their local Saturday brunch meeting in Marina del Rey.

I spoke about how WRS was my first networking meeting ever, how nervous I was, how I really didn't know how to craft a thirty-second commercial, and how I learned how to be effective by helping others and referring business to them. That in turn helped people get to know me and refer business to me.

Laura took a different tack. After praising WRS, she gave a terrific list of instructions, and I got her permission to share them with you (they will work for any networking group anywhere).

Laura Arnold's Top 10 Surefire Ways to Sabotage Yourself at WRS

1. Arrive late to meetings and leave before they end. (Extra credit: be disruptive when you do this.)
2. Take a long time to return phone calls, or better yet, don't return them at all.
3. Don't join any committees or do anything to increase your visibility in the organization.
4. Isolate yourself from colleagues in the same or related categories as yourself and never refer business to them.
5. Attend meetings sporadically or not at all.
6. Never refer business to other members or use their services or products.

7. Ignore WRS protocol. Hard sell to everybody whenever you get a chance.

8. Never meet with members before, after, or between meetings to build relationships.

9. Talk incessantly about yourself and never ask anyone about themselves or their businesses.

10. Be focused only on yourself and what's in it for you.

"I promise you, if you follow all or even most of these guidelines, you are *guaranteed* little or no business at WRS," she finished. The audience howled with laughter.

WRS has great training to teach you how to network effectively, and it's based on Zig Ziglar's saying, "You can have everything in life you want if you will just help enough other people get what they want."

The worst thing you can do is spend all this time and energy networking, speaking, and collecting business cards and then go home and put them in a file. Or add them to your mailing list without asking permission (that's spamming, you know). You networked to make connections, and the best connections are people you become friends with. What do you think needs to happen next for you to become friends? You have to spend some time talking with them—either on the phone, over coffee, or over lunch. Meaning you have to follow up with a phone call. Yes, sending an email or handwritten note will also be appreciated, but if you just send a note, are you hoping that they will take the initiative and call you?

Somebody has to go first, and if you're reading this, that somebody is you.

Rating Sheets or Intake Forms

When I speak at meetings, I always have handouts—usually a brochure, some article or bit of information on the topic, and a rating sheet. You want to be able to connect with the people who heard you speak and might be interested in your products or services, so you have to have some kind of intake form that they fill out with their contact information on it.

I include questions like "What was the best usable idea you gained from this program?" and "What do you wish there had been more time for?" followed by a checklist of their primary areas of concern. I list items such as "making more money," "paying off debt," "secrets of selling," and "building your business." You'll list things that are appropriate for your business.

After that, I have boxes to check that indicate the level of follow-up they would like, such as information on my workshops, how to become a certified Financial Stress Reduction coach, or if they know of another group that might book me as a speaker. At the end of the form, I put "Thank you! It has been a pleasure to serve you!"

You can modify this to suit your needs, listing the problems your customers encounter that you solve or the benefits you provide that they might want.

Admission of failure: for years I spoke, passed out my rating sheets, got nice laughs and wonderful applause…and nobody filled out the form. Well, one or two or five people out of fifty, but that's not good, is it?

I was embarrassed to ask for the forms at the end of the talk. I didn't ask for them with the same urgency as I spoke with about my topic, and I was always anxious and insecure about it.

Enlightenment happened one happy day when I was at a networking meeting and Jane Euler and Debra Lauzon of the law firm of Lauzon and Euler were giving a talk. They were terrific—warm, caring, generous, and savvy young female attorneys who specialized in employment and family law. I enjoyed their presentation very much.

They had placed a big bouquet of flowers on the table next to the podium where they gave their talk, and at the end of it, they said, "We've got some handouts for all of you, and an intake form. If you would please fill that out and turn it in to us, at the end of the meeting, we're going to have a drawing from these forms for this beautiful floral bouquet."

I watched wide-eyed while every single person in the room filled out their form and turned it in.

Well, dang! Why hadn't I thought of that? They certainly had, and I saw it worked, so like any good entrepreneur, I copied their idea and started having a drawing for a free gift at the end of my talks.

At that time, I hadn't written a book yet, so I gave away money. I started with a fifty-dollar bill and held it up at the end of my talk, saying, "I talk about money, so I'm putting my money where my mouth is and giving away this fifty-dollar bill. All you have to do is fill out the rating sheet and I'll pick one of them to win the fifty dollars."

One hundred percent of the audience filled out the form.

After a few talks, I wondered if I was giving away too much money and if it would work just as well with a twenty-dollar bill. Yep, it did. I remember one man put on his rating sheet under "Best usable idea" was my using the drawing to get fifty leads for only twenty dollars.

After *The Wealthy Spirit* was published, I gave away a free copy of the book instead of the money. I didn't get 100 percent of the audience with it, but I got something better: 100 percent of the people who were my *target market*, i.e., people who were interested in me and my products and services.

Branding: Your Difference That Makes A Difference

Branding is your company logo, mission statement, goals, attitudes, and symbols. For me, it began with my phrase "Financial Stress Reduction" and came to include the gold tennis shoes and gold nail polish I wear and some of the images and phrases I use. You create a brand to be instantly recognizable by your public.

One of my branded ideas is the analogy of sharks, dolphins, and tuna.

If you've been reading one of my books, my blog, or my newsletters for a while, you know I divide the world into three groups: dolphins, sharks, and tuna. Dolphins are happy, honest, and friendly. Sharks will do anything to eat you. Tuna are the blissfully ignorant victims swimming with the sharks and getting eaten.

You'll never make money working with sharks—they want all the money for themselves. You'll never make money working with tuna—they don't have any money. You've got to train to become a dolphin and swim with other dolphins to be happy, joyful, and rich—inside and out.

I didn't always know this. I was one of the tuna—I took on clients who couldn't pay me (tuna) or who didn't want to pay me (sharks). You see the problem.

I had to toughen up, make rules for my business, and abide by them. I had to get smart and maintain the profitability of my business. Then I could afford to be compassionate and help others as charitable giving—but not everyone and not all the time! Now I say I'm a tuna in recovery.

It's important that your clients, employees, or business associates feel special for being a part of your community. Mine all know that they are dolphins—happy, helpful, talented, and smart.

As an author, speaker, and coach, this analogy has served me well as part of my brand. People relate to these simple categories and share them with others. A woman at a conference put me on the phone with her husband. He was a college professor who enjoyed the sea creature categories and wanted to tell me so. "Sending out ships" has been positively identified with me also—a woman once called to tell me she overheard a woman say that phrase. She immediately went to her and said, "Do you know Chellie Campbell?" She did, and since they were both dolphins, they established a connection!

Earlier in this book I mentioned Lynne Azpeitia, the psychotherapist and coach who specializes in working with gifted and creative adults. I have met a lot of therapists who specialize in eating disorders, marriage and family issues, alcohol or drug treatment, depression, teenagers, and others. But Lynne was the first I heard mention gifted adults. What a great brand! When she gives her feedback, we all listen intently because she'll point out to us certain behaviors we are exhibiting that are typical of gifted people.

For example, someone asked how you would go about finding a good networking group when there are so many. I responded, "Google 'networking in Los Angeles,' see what shows up that looks interesting, and go to the meeting. While you're there, watch how people behave and how you feel in the room and see if it's a fit. Then look for the warmest, friendliest, happiest, most successful-looking dolphin-type person at the meeting, and ask them where else they network. Then go to those meetings."

Everyone thought that was a great idea, and Lynne jumped in to tell me that was a great piece of advice and should go into an article or a book. As I made a note about it, she said, "That's your genius, Chellie—these things just flow naturally from you. Gifted people aren't always aware of the things they say and do that are special because it's normal for them. They think everyone has ideas like that."

I looked at her and laughed. "Lynne, what a brilliant marketing niche you have invented. All your clients get to feel like they are gifted, creative, and a genius! I sure love getting feedback like that."

How do your clients feel about being a member of your community? If the answer isn't special, privileged, and creative, you might want to rethink your branding.

Social Media

Marketing your business has radically changed over the past twenty years and continues to shift with the advent of new social media platforms on the Internet. Back in the day before the Internet, I attended networking meetings, printed brochures, did mass mailings (oh, the postage and printing expenses!), and made innumerable telephone calls to prospective clients. I would speak at events, especially local networking meetings. I taught three classes per week, each with eight to twelve students, in my home. It was a really simple business model with just a few tasks that I did repeatedly—I went to eight to twelve networking meetings a month and made fifty to seventy-five phone calls a week.

I attend fewer in-person networking meetings now. Because of all the networking I did early in my business, my books sold well. That helped my reach expand beyond Los Angeles, across the country, and even internationally. Instead of brochures, I maintain and update my website; send several marketing emails plus one newsletter every month; read and respond to fifty to one hundred incoming emails per day; write a blog; post daily on LinkedIn, Twitter, and Facebook; correspond with clients, prospective clients, and colleagues; do radio, magazine, and teleclass interviews; and speak at events. Instead of teaching classes in person in Los Angeles, which only people who live within driving distance can attend, I give teleclasses that can reach people all over the world.

Even though there are so many time-savers created by the Internet—such as sending a reminder note to my clients with one email instead of making twenty individual phone calls—sometimes my business today seems like a lot more work…and the potential for even more work is endless! But I remember being told "work will expand to fill the time you're willing to devote to it," so I make sure to keep work within certain boundaries and then go out to play.

Networking on Facebook, Pinterest, Google+, Twitter, etc.

So many people have jumped on the social media advertising bandwagon these days that sometimes it seems just like a television station broadcasting commercials all day long. I found I wasn't very interested in reading endless pitches to buy people's products or services. What was interesting was to engage in conversations about a topic and become friends with people.

It's just like joining a live networking group. If all you do is try to sell your products and services, it's not going to work. You need to engage with other people and be interested in them and what they're doing. Read their blog and comment. Share other people's interesting posts with your friends. Sign up for someone else's teleclass and send them a testimonial if you enjoyed it. Refer them business if you can.

When you're interested in others, others will be interested in you. Simple, no?

Here are some Facebook statistics, which came from Dale Collie at SpeakerNet News, as quoted by Vickie Sullivan in her email newsletter "Tips, Trends, & Tirades," in 2014:

- Posts with questions generate 70 percent more comments than the average post. Other top producers: clever language (120 percent increase) and asking for input (also a 120 percent increase).
- Passionate debates and touching, emotional stories generate two to three times the increase in feedback.

- Checking in happens around the workday: morning, noon, after work, and late at night.

The bottom line is that when you show up anywhere—in person, on the web, in a video or podcast—be yourself and share interesting stories or useful facts. I read many self-help books, and the advice is usually the same. Only the personal stories are different, and when I read a new book, that's what I'm looking for—engaging personal stories that illustrate a principle, not just another laundry list of "do this, don't do that." When reading Facebook posts, I want to get to know the people behind the posts. Friendships develop from that, and business too.

Expanding Your Reach—But Not Too Far

Writing this in January 2014, I googled "financial stress reduction" and I was second on the first page out of 4.6 million websites. I googled "financial stress." There were 140 million websites…and I was right up there on the second page. (Be still my heart—the SEO is working.)

This was pretty exciting news for me, and of course, a ranking like this didn't happen overnight. It's the culmination of sending out a lot of little ships—building a website; having a membership group, forums, audio, video, and lots of written content; establishing a presence on Facebook, LinkedIn, and Twitter; and writing a daily blog.

Sounds exhausting, doesn't it? And it can be too, unless you pace yourself. You can't do everything every day. Entrepreneurs can work 24-7 and not get everything done. We're great at endlessly thinking up stuff to do—another program, seminar, product, marketing campaign, publicity, another book to write, another online group to join—the possibilities are endless!

And no, you can't do it all. You can't even do most of it. You can only do a fraction. So you have to make peace with that fact and just do a little bit every day.

I spoke with a woman who was interested in publishing her book but was overwhelmed with all the work it would take. I agreed with her that it was a lot of work. But so what? You can't think like that. If you look at the totality of a project and all it will take to accomplish your goal, it can be so daunting that you don't even want to start!

Look at the end result and just send out a small ship today. All your little bits of work will, over time, add up to a big accomplishment! Focus on your goal and get started. I promise, you'll be amazed at what you can do.

I remember when I was younger and hadn't accomplished much, I would often read books or listen to speeches given by high-powered successful women who had big laundry lists of awards and accomplishments. Now so many years and so much hard work later, I have a bit of a laundry list of my own. And now I know what it really means—it just means you're old! Give yourself a break—with time and effort, your rewards and acknowledgments will come too. But the truth is your rewards come every day with the people you help. Nothing feels better than a compliment from a grateful client!

Selling Is Serving

When you think about selling, do you get excited and happy? Do you look forward to calling a prospective client who just might buy your products and services?

Or do you wrinkle your nose, back away, shake your head, and think, "That's the worst part of being in my own business"?

I asked Joel Libava, The Franchise King, what the number one reason was that most business owners were unsuccessful. He answered bluntly, "They can't sell." Nancy Sardella told me about her experience attempting to franchise her networking business: "I sold franchises all over the country," she said. "I trained them on all the systems and gave them a complete script for how to make sales calls to get members. And they still couldn't do it. I ended up closing the franchises and focused on running my own local operation."

One reason many small business owners can't sell is because they have the wrong attitude about selling. They think a sales call is asking people to give them money. When you're in a helping profession, making a call to someone to ask for money is hardly an empowering psychological position.

But they have it backward. Selling is what you do to serve the customer. You are searching for the people who need what you have and helping them have it. There are people who need you but they don't know who to hire and they are afraid of making a mistake. Making a sales call is a sacrifice you make on behalf of someone else out of your sincere desire to help them.

George Clooney knows this secret to success. In a 2011 article by David Gergen in *Parade*, he said, "I was a baseball player in school. I had a good arm, I could catch anything, but I was having trouble hitting. I would be like, 'I wonder if I'll hit it; just let me hit the ball.' And then I went away for the fall, learned how to hit, and by my sophomore year I'd come to the plate and think, 'I wonder where I want to hit the ball, to the left or right?' Just that little bit of skill and confidence changed everything. Well, I had to treat acting like that. I had to stop going to auditions thinking, 'Oh, I hope they like me.' I had to go in thinking I was the answer to their problem. You could feel the difference in the room immediately."

Make Gold Calls, Not Cold Calls

Cold calling sounds like what it is—harsh and cold. But since I say, "the money is in the phone," I call it "gold calling." I painted gold dollar signs on my telephone with my gold nail polish too. They remind me that I'd better call people if I want to have any clients in my business. All the money you want is waiting for you at the other end of the phone, but you have to pick it up and reach out and touch someone.

Cold calling works. But the percentage of sales is very small in relation to the number of calls you have to make. So I prefer to network. Then all of my calls are gold calls. I've met these people already and we have a mutual interest in each other. This is a much easier phone call to make than a cold call to someone you don't know.

Making calls to people after a networking event is the single most important action missing from most business owners' game plan. They are happy to go to the meetings, eat, and say hello to people. They think the idea is to give everyone their business card. They have the illusion that if people are interested, they will call.

But wait, you might be thinking. Phone calls are old technology. Can't I just get all my customers through advertising on Facebook and Twitter and sending emails?

No. Not if it's just more pitching.

Oh, you can get some. You can get followers and readers, and eventually some of them may turn into clients. But the truth that no one wants to tell you is that it's a very low percentage and it's really *slow*. Don't you get hundreds of emails, tweets, and posts every day? Do you read them all? Do you know the average open rate of an email newsletter is only 10 to 15 percent? Your copy had better be really great, and you'd better have thousands of people on your list if you're going to rely on that.

The real secret to social networking online is the same as physical networking in person—you have to create relationships. And you don't do that by endless pitching. The tweets and posts have to engage the reader, reveal yourself and what you're about, and show your caring and expertise.

Here's an example.

Lucy, an attorney in Texas and a participant in one of my tele-classes, said her buying process went like this: she had signed up for my newsletter, read it for months, and then signed up for my 365 daily pages from *The Wealthy Spirit*. As she read them each day, so many of them spoke to her that she started printing them out and putting them in a notebook. When she got so many the notebook was messy, she decided to just buy the book. When I announced in my newsletter that I was having a free teleclass, she signed up for it and listened. She wrote me to say thank you and that she enjoyed every minute of it, and she was interested in signing up for my workshop. That's when I called her and closed the sale.

So when you do get a call from someone who is interested in your product or service, how are you going to convince them that *you* are the one they should work with? Do you know what to say to close the deal when they are really interested but they have objections? Like time and money and "I have to ask my husband"?

What are the secrets to having wonderful, engaging phone conversations with prospective clients that result in higher ticket sales?

In the next chapter, I will give you specific steps and specific questions to ask to help you make gold calls instead of cold calls and close more sales.

It's Not Cold Calling—
It's Gold Calling

One of the things that stops women financially is that, culturally, we aren't trained to ask for money. Try saying "I love to ask for money" and see how that feels. Yucky, right? Try this one: "People love to give me money!" That usually feels pretty good. That's because we want it, but we want it given to us—we don't want to have to ask. But in the marketplace, we have to ask—for a raise, a promotion, the business from a client. And then we have to set our price and ask for that!

You see the problem.

Asking for the business was a tough one for me initially. And then I learned the secret of how to make a great phone call that resulted in business…

Nope, not every call. But enough. I've used the phone to sell millions of dollars of workshop enrollments over the past twenty-plus years.

I can feel your eyes rolling now. You're probably thinking that the last thing you want to do is become a telemarketer. But what if you just call to make a friend? Then if they indicate an interest in what you do, you can take the next step and tell them about it.

I know. You want all the advertising you do to work and just have people sign up to buy without having to talk with you. You want them to click the Buy button on your website. You want people to call *you* and say they want to buy your product or service.

In the immortal words of Dr. Phil, "So how's that working for ya?"

That strategy will work for a few small sales, but for the big-ticket items, potential clients and customers want to talk with you. They want to know that you understand them, where they're coming from, and what they want. They want to know that you've worked with someone in their business before or someone who has the problems they have. They want to know you're not a scammer trying to get their money but leaving them with nothing at the end of the process. *They need you to coach them through the buying process.* Because marketing doesn't close the sale.

People see your ads, emails, posts, etc. but don't often stop to read them. When they do (which could take months or years), you'll definitely get some interest in your work—people will love your content and want more. But then they may just wait for all the free stuff and never buy anything. Sound familiar?

"The money is in the phone!"

I've been saying that for years. I know I have some really good content, and a lot of people have told me that mine is the only email newsletter they subscribe to anymore. The books have been wonderful for publicizing my work—one insurance salesman I met on Facebook told me he had been reading a page a day of *The Wealthy Spirit* for eight years. It's wonderful to have fans who read your articles, newsletters, social media posts, ads, and books.

But most of them won't pick up the phone to call me, because it's hard to call a stranger and you don't know how you will be received. So you need to be the generous, brave soul who picks up the phone and reaches out to them.

All my sales happen after the marketing. They happen when I call people after I give a speech or a free teleclass or meet them at a networking event.

If you skip this step, you're not only going to leave most of your prospective clients unfulfilled and underserved, but you'll also leave buckets of cash behind everywhere you go! They won't take the risk to buy your product or service that will benefit them, and you won't get the money you need to continue to be in business.

That's a lose-lose transaction.

The Email Marketing Funnel Doesn't Always Work

One summer, I enrolled in a teleclass on how to make a lot of money teaching teleclasses. The woman was bright and personable and had demonstrated making a significant income as a coach. I had already transitioned my business from in-person workshops in Los Angeles to teleclasses where students could attend from anywhere in the world, since my books had achieved some recognition and people were asking me to provide this service. But I figured I could learn something new, and I got a lot of value from the strategies and suggestions she made.

She had set up an online forum where her participants could try out some of her strategies, like coming up with a snazzy title that would draw people in and writing sizzling email copy. It was great practice, and I enjoyed giving and receiving feedback. I met some other great coaches I admired and respected.

At the end of the class, the forum was going to shut down. But a number of us didn't want to stop, so someone suggested we create a Facebook group for the lot of us who wanted to continue to interact, exchange information, and support each other.

Over the next couple of years, we enjoyed the supportive interactions, terrific information, and joint ventures that resulted from our group. But eventually, a number of people reported that although they followed the course instructions, created their hooky titles, gave a great free teleclass to advertise, and followed up with terrifically written emails advertising their for-fee classes, they had not gotten the number of buyers they wanted. One woman reported getting 700 people registered for her free teleclass, with 150 actually attending the live call (the rest got the recording afterward), yet she hardly got any buyers for her paid program.

"Would love to get stats from the rest of you on the effectiveness of the preview call system," she posted to our group. "What's working for you? What's not? I am deeply desiring energy efficiency— energy that I've invested (time and money) and seeing direct returns on that investment."

I chimed in to the conversation with my perspective on emails versus calling:

My last free teleclass was about networking and gold calling. My FreeConferencing.com service sends me a list of the phone numbers of the people who attended the teleclass. A lot of people were really tickled by the fact that I practiced what I preached, and we had great conversations. I just started with, "Hi, thanks so much for being on the call…how did you find out about it… what do you do…how long have you been doing that…how's the economy affecting you…" etc. It's different with everyone, but you want to get them talking. They'll share and eventually want to know how your program will work for them specifically. When you answer that, then you have to "close" them, but when you come from service and really wanting to help them, it doesn't feel pushy, even though you are indeed pushing them to make a decision for their highest good, see?

It is true that when I talk with people, a lot of them have been reading my book, emails, etc. for years and often wanted to take my class but it's expensive yada yada—look guys, they are afraid to call you! So you have to call them. One woman I spoke with had been reading The Wealthy Spirit *every day since 2006 but still didn't enroll in class until I called her and spoke with her.*

You probably have hundreds of people out there who have enjoyed your programs and want more but are just afraid to take action and need some guidance to make the decision. You're the star of the show, and they are happy to hear from you!

To answer your questions about the time/energy it takes to make the phone calls—it's not that hard, and as a matter of fact, it's fun! I think of "selling" as "coaching" someone to take the action step that will improve their life. If you're a coach, you can coach people to buy. It's easy. Really, you just call to make a friend and let it proceed from there, but your purpose has to be to enroll the person so that you can help them (not everyone, just those you truly believe you can help).

I always have a lot of people on my "interest list" that I start follow-up calls with about five to six weeks before class starts. I keep a phone log so I know my stats. With these calls to the already interested, I made forty-two calls (phone dials) and actually spoke with nineteen people and enrolled five in my next telecourse.

After the free teleclass, in three weeks I made 126 calls, spoke with fifty-eight people, and sold ten, with fourteen interested for the next one. That's 17 percent sold or 41 percent if you count the ones who want to come next year. I'm thrilled with that.

Most coaches don't make calls—they rely on the information in their free teleclasses and follow-up emails to sell their products and services. But my service is very personal, and I want to have a connection with each member of the small interactive group who takes my class.

Practically everyone was completely surprised by my call but happy to talk with me, which was wonderful. I was delighted to chat with them and get to know them and start a relationship. Some people seemed suspicious, as in "Is this a sales call; I don't want to be pressured into anything" and got off the phone right away. One man hung up on me (maybe it was his wife who was on my call). Ouch!

But then I thought, "Not my people—next!"

When you make calls, you don't know what you're going to get. You can't take it personally—it's not about you. You're reaching out to help people, but you don't know who needs you. So when someone is rude or inhospitable, just blow it off. So what? There are a zillion more people to call…

Some people sign up right away, and some wait for later, and of course, some people will never actually take my class. That's always the way it is when you're in business and selling your products and services. But the secret is this: if you make enough calls, enough people will buy from you, and you'll make the money you want.

Somebody Needs Your Help

I put a sign near my phone. It says: "Somebody needs your help!" Make one for yourself. That's what makes it easy for me to make the calls. That's what keeps me calling. I think of all the people who have been helped by my work, who are happier and more successful, and who send me lovely notes of thanks and blessings. Putting myself out there, making calls to people, is the sacrifice I make on their behalf. Women are generally pretty good at sacrificing themselves on behalf of others. So get to it! That idea should help you.

If you're in a personal service business, you've got to reach out to your potential clients. You can't just rely on emails or ads or websites or other marketing. After a while, all the buzz words and snazzy phrases all begin to sound alike. Everyone promises the same benefits—who are you going to believe really delivers?

After the economy crashed in 2008, it seemed to me like every life coach in America had suddenly become a money coach. I got emails from many of them, and every one said versions of the same thing: "I'll help you make more money," "I'll help you get more clients," "I'll help you make a six-figure income." How many different ways can you say those things?

The things that differentiate you from your competition are your personality, your experience, your stories, and the success stories of the people you've helped. People won't know you are the one who's the real deal unless you call them.

Here's a note I received from one woman I called:

I'm one of those people who listened to your teleconference and was surprised and pleased that you picked up the phone to contact me afterward. I've thought a lot about our conversation since then. It still makes me smile to know that you practice the techniques that you tell people about. I can't say that's true about a lot of people I get solicitations from on a regular basis. Generally they send me emails telling me how great their training program is and how I'll fail if I don't participate in this program. I'm required to reach out to them if I want more information or to sign up. They never take the time to find out whether the program is even a good fit for me or something I might use in my own classes. Shame on them!

You demonstrated what to do to get business. You took the time to talk with me and learn about what my needs are…so thanks for calling me and getting to know me. I appreciate that you "walk the walk" and not just "talk the talk." I hope we have the chance to talk again sometime!

I loved that!

People may want what you have, but they need to talk to you to see if what you have can truly help them, to see if you've ever helped someone in their situation, and to feel secure about making the investment of time and money in your services. They want to know that you want to help them personally. They want to feel you care about them.

Some seminar leaders who are tremendously charismatic can close people en masse in a group. That is a rare talent. But anyone can have a caring conversation with one person and convince them to buy.

Sure, the marketing I do is effective too—I'm not suggesting you don't need to do that. Many of the people who enroll have been reading *The Wealthy Spirit*, my newsletters, blogs, etc. for years, so they know me and my work and what I stand for and believe in.

But they enroll in my classes on the phone.

How many people do you imagine you might have helped if you had just reached out and called them? How much better off would they have been if you had helped them? How much better off would *you* have been if you had that many more clients?

If you don't make the call, you're leaving your prospect alone to make the decision of whether your service will help them. They are going to sit with all their objections—time, energy, money—and their fear of spending money on something that won't work. They need you to point out the future benefits they will have after working with you that will far outweigh their objections. Who knows that better than you?

You see why I think the money is in the phone?

The Alchemy of Gold Calls

This is my personal step-by-step guide to successfully gold calling warm prospects I have met while networking on Facebook, through referrals, online, etc. This is the exact process I have been using for years to build my workshops into a successful six-figure income seminar business, while taking lots of time off to play and have fun.

Many people go to networking groups, hand out their business cards, and then go back to their office and wait for the phone to ring—and then they wonder why they're broke. If it was that easy to make sales, everyone would be doing it. No, *you* have to pick up the phone and make it ring in other people's offices.

You may need to rewrite some of the details of this guide to meet the needs of your specific business, but some version of it will work for you. Watch out when the "yeah, but" in your head says "Oh, but my business is different," "That won't work for me," or "It's against the ethics of my profession to make a sales call." You're not calling to make a sale. You're calling to make a friend and get to know a fellow networker so you can refer business to each other. You're calling to create a circle of influence with other business owners. It's just a side benefit that when you make a lot of these calls, you make a lot of sales in the process too.

The most important thing to note before you start is that this process is for win-win negotiations. This is not to be used for "smashing and grabbing," like a thief who smashes a window, grabs some goodies, and runs off. If you don't really like or care about the person you are calling, it is going to show and you're going to sound phony. Be real, genuine, and friendly; the worst that can happen is you make a new friend.

It's really easy to make gold calls, if you do it right. And yes, of course it takes some learning and experience to get good at it. So what? Doesn't everything? Did you play a musical instrument perfectly the first time you picked it up? Did you play tennis or basketball perfectly the first time out on the court?

No. You had to take lessons, practice, fail, and try again, over and over, until you improved. When I was learning how to make gold calls, I made lots of mistakes and missed a lot of sales I would have made if I was better at it. But I figured there were so many potential people to call it would be okay if I blew off one hundred of them learning how to do it. I knew if I didn't learn it, I was going to go broke and have to get a *job*.

That was a fate worse than making bad phone calls for a while until I got better at it. See? Fear can be a really great motivator.

The following section is my step-by-step formula for making a gold call, including who to call, how to find them, feeling positive, finding rapport, the magic question you must ask, sharing the benefits of your product or service, asking for the order, asking for the money, overcoming objections, when to let them off the hook, what to do if the customer says no, what to do after the sale, getting referrals and testimonials, cultivating centers of influence, handling cancellations, and following up.

This formula works beautifully for sole practitioners, home-based business owners, independent contractors, freelancers, and network marketers of all kinds. I've taught it to salespeople, chiropractors, coaches, massage therapists, attorneys, accountants, people who sell gift baskets, clothing, advertising specialties, and many others.

If you aren't in your own business, you can revise these steps so you can get volunteers for the school bake sale, raise funds for a charity, get out the vote for your favorite politician, or ask someone on a date. Gold calling skills will help you in every area of your life.

1. Who are you going to call?

There are about twenty million people in the greater Los Angeles area, where I live and work. That's twenty million prospects who might love to buy my products or services! How many people are in your area? If you have an Internet business or a business with products, the whole world could be your customer. You can start cold calling everybody one by one, or you can create warm calls for yourself by being out and about at networking meetings, parties, social events, or on Facebook, LinkedIn, Twitter, Google+, and Pinterest, making contacts.

Don't we all love to be loved? It's easy to call people who you already know love you. It's more difficult reaching out to people who haven't heard of you, who don't know you, who don't yet trust or believe you can help them, who raise all the objections of time and money and family obligations. They've got to remodel their house first, and they'll take your course and learn to make money and have fun later. Sigh.

But that's the work all of us face, isn't it? We want to help others and they need our help, but they need convincing. They need you to guide them to their highest good, but they aren't buying until you guide them to invest in the process—spiritually, physically, emotionally, and financially. I teach people how to master their money, and what's the first obstacle we encounter? Money. It's too funny, really.

Many people have financial issues they want to solve, but only a few will put their time, money, and energy into the work it takes to solve it. Many people need accountants, attorneys, chiropractors, nutritionists, speech coaches, music teachers, cooking teachers, and party planners. How are you going to find them and then convince them that out of all the people who provide the same service, *you* are the one they need?

Who and Where Is Your Target Market?

Know your target market and go to the places where they hang out. You can network anytime, anywhere, and make wonderful contacts. There are many business networking groups in every city. If you can't find one, start one. But you don't have to restrict yourself to business organizations. Parties are unofficial networking groups. Social clubs or social networks, charities with fundraising activities—the possibilities are endless.

You never know what event can turn into a networking opportunity. You can network while in line at the grocery store, while pumping gas at the gas station, while riding in an elevator. My networking even paid off when I was on jury duty. The judge said, "It would be nice for all of us to get to know each other. Let's go around the room and everyone say their name and what they do for a living." I was amazed—we were going to do thirty-second commercials on jury duty!

So when it was my turn, I said, "I'm Chellie Campbell, and I treat money disorders—spending bulimia and income anorexia." There was a shout of laughter at that, and I held up my book (always prepared for book promotion, I had copies of my book with me, of course) and said, "I'm also the author of the book *The Wealthy Spirit*."

I sold five books.

You never know when networking is going to pay off. I've sold my book to telemarketers who called to sell me something. I bought a ring watch off the Internet, and the seller wrote me a cheerful note, so I wrote her back and suggested she might enjoy my book. She emailed me an hour later:

> Chellie, I just went in and read a few of the pages on Amazon—what a great book!! I'm going to buy it and I think I'll get one for my son too—no, I know I'll get one for my son too, lol. Thanks so much, Elaine, Glitz Galore.

Now, isn't that fun? You never know what great people might be out there unless you reach out and share a bit of yourself along the way. Why not strike up a conversation with someone new today? You may be surprised with the results.

2. Start with a positive attitude!

Now that you've met a lot of people and have gotten their names and phone numbers, you have to pick up the phone and call them. Make sure you are in a happy frame of mind and are smiling—a smile can be heard in your voice. An energetic attitude and a sincere positive belief that your product or service truly helps people will give you the passion, drive, and persistence needed to sell it success-fully. Think positive and practice positive statements out loud! Here are a few samples:

- "People love to give me money!"
- "People are enjoying the process of making me rich!"
- "I am a money-making machine, and I'm making a lot of it today!"
- "I love my life!"

If you just can't get the energy up today, that's what paperwork is for. You can always try again tomorrow.

Picking up the phone to make a call to someone you don't know well, hoping to "turn your contact into a contract" as my friend and sales trainer, Ike Krieger, likes to say, is one of the most difficult things for people to do. But if you want to make any money, you have to do it. You must reframe your attitude about selling to think of it as having fun and building friendships.

I call the sales process "sending out ships" so that one day your ship can come in. First you build the shipyard—that's your business plan, your website, and your service or product. Next, you turn on the light in the lighthouse to let people know who and where you are. This includes all your marketing activities—emails, blogs, arti-cles, speeches, networking, and social media. Sending out ships is your sales process—making phone calls to people who might buy your product or service or to arrange a meeting with someone who might buy it. Then you follow up the ships you've sent out with flares, tugboats, the coast guard, and the navy, if necessary, to guide them to your dock.

You can't send out one ship and wait. Sometimes they turn out to be a slow boat to China or the *Pirates of the Caribbean* get them or there's a *Mutiny on the Bounty* or they sink like the *Titanic*. But your fortune is made when the *Golden Hind*, *Robert E. Lee*, *Allure of the Seas*, or the *History Supreme* (look *that* one up!) arrive with all the riches you desire.

Send those ships out every day. Then one day you'll be unloading your treasures!

3. Find rapport with the prospect.

A friend who listened to me make some sales calls one afternoon said, "Chellie, you have an amazing ability with people on the phone. You always sound like you care about them."

I said, "Yes, well—there's a trick to that."

His ears pricked up at that. "What is the trick?" he asked excitedly.

"I really do care," I answered.

The sales method I am teaching you here is how to sell to people you believe you can help. This isn't to be used to "zap" people. The problem with zapping people is that you can only do it one time— then you have to find new people to zap. That makes you work a lot harder than if you find the people who will truly love and benefit from your product or service, and then you aren't trying to zap them—you are showing them all the reasons why you believe your service will improve their lives. If you don't have integrity in this process, it may work for you in the beginning, but it will fall apart quickly. Karma wins.

I don't really create rapport with the prospect—I *find* rapport. The best approach in calling a prospect is to have a sincere interest in them. If you naturally like people, you are ahead of the game. If you don't, develop a liking for people. Or go live on the moon.

Being able to have a good sales conversation is a skill everyone needs to develop. You might be selling your product or service, or you may just be convincing your child to pick up their room or a friend to go with you to a movie you want to see.

The biggest mistake most people make is that they start with an "I" message. As in "I want to see this movie; do you want to come with me?" or "I'm a coach with twenty years' experience and here are my credentials…"

I tell all my clients to start a sales conversation by making a new friend. Be sincerely interested in them! This cannot be faked. If you aren't truly interested in the person you're talking to, they can tell. Can't you? Don't you remember some fake, schmaltzy salesperson who was acting as though he liked you but you knew he had an agenda to sell you his stuff and he really wasn't listening to you? Most people are really bad actors.

Be friendly, upbeat, and conversational. Focus on them first, not yourself. Ask about their business, how long they've been doing it, what they did before, what they're doing to get more business, where they network, who their target market is, what kind of clients they're looking for. Ask them where they grew up, what their hobbies are, what they do for fun, etc. These are all "first date" questions—questions you would ask anyone before getting involved in a relationship.

You are looking for points of contact, similar interests, things you would look for in a friend. You're not only getting to know them better and how you might serve them through your product or service, but also actively looking for some help you can give them right now. If you can give them some referrals or invite them to a networking group that might be helpful to them, do that right away. They will appreciate you, and that is a great way to start a relationship.

When you make gold calls, you're hoping to connect with your people. You know who your people are—their faces light up when they see you. Don't you love that? You can tell who they are when you call them too. I was making gold calls on my gold phone one day and two calls really stuck out in my mind.

Call number one: "Hi, this is Chellie," I said when the woman—I'll call her Sheila—answered the phone.

"Yes?" she said flatly.

Thinking she didn't remember me, I said, "I spoke at the meeting last month—I'm the author of *The Wealthy Spirit*…"

"I know who you are," she broke in. Then silence.

Ugh. I could just tell by the tone of her voice that she wasn't delighted to hear from me. It was time to cut this conversation short. This is the prescription for doing that: ask them if they want to buy your service before you've spent any time with them, they will say "no thanks," and you can hang up. In this case, I briefly explained to Sheila that I had a class coming up and would she be interested in receiving some information about it. Right on cue, she said, "No thanks," and we were done.

Call number two: "Hi, this is Chellie," I said to Amber.

"Oh, my goodness, really? I am so delighted to hear from you!" she bubbled. "You're wonderful! I am so glad you called!"

Ah, isn't that just what you want to hear? The door was open for a wonderful conversation, and yes, she was interested in my class too.

So how long does it take you to figure out if someone is happy you called?

4. Ask the magic question!

Eventually, after you've asked all these questions about them, they will ask about you. "So tell me about your workshop," they'll say to me.

If I start talking about my workshop now, I'm going to sink this ship. What am I going to tell them it's about? Debt reduction? That's fine if their credit cards are charged to the max, but what if they have no debt? Am I going to say it's about learning to sell? What if they don't sell anything? In either case, they'll think my workshop isn't for them. I don't know what this customer wants or needs. I have to identify the pleasure they want to have or the pain they want to alleviate. I have to ask what I call "the magic question." The magic question for my financial workshop is: "What would you like to change about money in your life?"

Because I've spent some time with them already, and they've answered many questions about themselves, their business, and their lives, they answer this one too. We have rapport, and they are in the habit of answering my questions. "Oh, I've decided to take early retirement and start a business, and I need to know how to do that." "I've got way too much debt, and I never seem to be able to get my credit cards paid off." "I really want to save more money." Do you think they would answer a question this personal if I started off the conversation like this: "Hi, this is Chellie. I met you last week. Would you like to tell me where you are the most screwed up with money so I can help you?"

What might your magic question be? If you're in one of the healing professions, you could ask, "If you could change anything related to your health, what would it be?" If you sell insurance, you might mention a recent disaster that's been in the news and then ask, "Do you feel secure that you are covered for any problem or disaster that might occur?" If you are a travel agent, how about asking, "What's the best vacation you ever had?" followed by "What's your dream vacation you haven't taken yet?" If you're a mortgage broker, you could start with "Do you own any real estate?" and if they say yes, you could follow that with "Are you thrilled with your current interest rate and the service you are getting from your broker?"

Remember that the first thing on the prospective customer's mind is "WIIFM"—"What's in it for me?" The most important thing to remember is that if *you're* talking, you're just talking, but if *they're* talking, you're selling. If people open up and talk about their real concerns and share with you what they really want, you can let them know how you can help them get that. Take copious notes during this process so that you can refer back to your prospect's specific problems or concerns later in this conversation or in subsequent conversations if they aren't ready to buy today. A salesman giving a seminar once told me that only 3 percent of the people you talk to are ready to buy today, but 33 percent will be ready to buy within ninety days. So you are going to need to call most people more than once.

5. Share the benefits and success stories of your product or service.

Now that you know what this particular person needs, you can focus on how you alleviate the pain they have or give them the pleasure they want. If you can't help them, if what you have isn't what they need, refer them to someone you know who can. (That's sending a ship into someone else's harbor. You won't make a sale with them today, but they will remember that you helped them, and when they need what you have later, they will be back.)

If someone tells me they want to learn more about the stock market and investing, I tell them that's not what I do and refer them to people who do what they need. But if I have the answer to their problems, I happily tell them everything I can that will motivate them to sign up for my class. This is where it is important to tell testimonial stories of other people who had their same problems or wanted the same benefits and the success they had with your product or service. These should be true, detailed stories that are fun, uplifting, exciting, or show amazing results.

If the prospect starts to warm to the idea of buying your product or service, they will start giving buying signals such as these: "How much does it cost?" "When do you do it?" "How long will it take?" "Have you ever worked with anyone in my situation before?" "Does it really work?" Or the question you really want to hear—"Do you take MasterCard or Visa?"

Then you can proceed to Step 6.

6. Ask for the order!

By now it should be clear if this person is a hot prospect and may buy. If the conversation has been going well and they've been giving you buying signals, you can ask them if they'd like to buy. This can be a little confrontational, since it asks them to say yes or no, so instead, I like to use what salespeople know as the "alternative of choice" close. I call it the "Do you want a red one or a blue one?" close. Instead of asking the prospect for a yes or a no, ask them which one of several options they want. For example, in selling my workshops, when I get to that point where the customer is leaning toward yes, I ask them if Mondays or Wednesdays work better for them. Then they're looking in the calendar to see when they can do it rather than thinking about whether to do it. It is a subtle but powerful difference! If they say "Mondays look good," I say, "Great! I'll put you in the Monday group." Then I go directly to Step 7.

7. Ask for the money!

The next thing to ask is "How would you like to pay for this?" This is a great question because it's another one of the "Do you want a red one or a blue one?" variety. You can tell them you take cash, check, and credit cards or will set up a payment plan or whatever your terms are. *It isn't a sale until you've gotten the money.* It is best to get a credit card number immediately when they say yes. People are much more likely to stay committed when they have paid. If possible, get the entire amount up front. Often people will suggest 50 percent deposit and the balance on delivery—you have to know what your terms are and if you will negotiate those terms upon occasion.

If they don't want to use a credit card but want to send a check, ask if they can send it today. Create a sense of urgency. Why should they buy today? There's not enough for everyone, or there's a discount if you buy today, etc. If they can't send a check today, ask them when they can send it and let them know you are putting it in your calendar for that day. If you don't get it within a day or two of that date, call them back—they might have encountered an objection/problem/concern or they're just scared to make the commitment. People don't like to call you with bad news, so you may never know they've decided to cancel until it's too late unless you have this follow-up system in place.

I learned this the hard way.

In the beginning of my workshop business, I used to be so delighted when someone said yes that I thanked them and got off the phone right away to celebrate. I'd send them an enrollment package with instructions about how to get here, a request for payment, etc. But I was afraid to ask the scary question about getting the money, so I didn't get the money. Funny how half of the people who said they were coming didn't show up the day of the class.

That made me so mad—and so broke.

Get the money now. If they aren't going to pay you now, they most likely aren't going to pay you later either. This is when they'll tell you "I have to ask my husband" or "I have to check my budget." This means they are not yet clear on the value of your product or service.

8. Overcome objections.

Sometimes when you ask for the order, people aren't yet ready to buy. They start coming up with all the reasons why they can't or shouldn't buy your product or service. This should be regarded as a sign that they need help allowing themselves to buy this. Otherwise, they'd give you a clear "no thanks, I'm not interested" and get off the phone. I don't advocate selling anything to anyone who doesn't really need it or want it. If you hard sell something to someone who really doesn't want it, they will be unhappy with you and whatever it is you're selling. You will be seen as a hard salesperson, and this prospect will likely bad-mouth you every chance they get.

But many legitimately interested prospects will talk themselves out of buying just because human beings are creatures of habit and buying this new thing will take them out of their usual habit. People are resistant to change and this is a change, so they often need a little coaxing. Remember, this is only if you can sense that the person will truly benefit from having this product or service and be happy with it once they've got it. If you sincerely believe that this person will benefit, then it is *your duty to them* as well as yourself to help them past their objections.

The two standard objections are time and money. You will need to write out specific answers to these objections. Acknowledge the problem and that you understand it's a problem. But then, wouldn't it be worth the money to have whatever the benefit is that they said they wanted? You can refer to your notes about the specific things that excited them about your product or service. You want to reinforce the benefits they've said they want. Then ask if this particular objection was handled, would they want to have the product or service? If they say yes, then you work on overcoming the specific objection.

Examples are helpful, so here are some of my responses to objections I encounter when selling my workshops:

1. **Time:** "I'm so overwhelmed! I have too much on my plate and not enough hours in the day!"

Who isn't overwhelmed these days? It's endemic in our society, with cell phones, social media, texting, and email allowing people to reach us 24-7. What is the reason you will give them that they should make room for your product or service?

I let them know that there are 168 hours in every week and my workshop is only two hours. That puts it in perspective right there, and they usually laugh. Then I ask them if it might be worth two hours a week for just eight weeks for them to make more money and achieve whatever financial goal it is they want. Yes, the class takes eight weeks, but how long have they had the problem they're experiencing? If that problem was solved or the benefit they want was obtained, wouldn't it be worth it? If they want to make more money, do they want to make more money right now, or do they want to make more money six months from now?

2. **Money:** "Oh, your course is too expensive!"

This is a common objection and one you're likely to hear often if you have a high-ticket product or service to sell. People have a certain amount of money coming in and it's mostly allocated already to their budgeted expenses. You just aren't on their budget yet. So they need help in seeing how they could afford you. What do they have to do without in order to buy your product or service? And would it be worth it if they do?

I acknowledge that the class is expensive—in comparison to eating lunch tomorrow. But think about it compared to your annual income for the last ten years. Now think about the annual income you'd like to have for the next ten years. Wouldn't it be worth this amount of money to increase your income 20 percent? Or 30 percent or 50 percent? I've had people in my workshop double their income in just eight weeks.

I reinforce that the course comes with a 100 percent money-back guarantee: They are better off financially in sixty days or their money back. How can they lose? And until they learn something new and break out of old financial habit patterns, how is their financial situation going to improve? If they don't do this program, what are they going to do instead that they think will work better?

I ask them if they lost $2,500, would it drastically change their life or lifestyle? But if they were able to increase their earning power 10, 20, or 30 percent for the rest of their life, would that drastically change their life or lifestyle? This puts it in perspective.

If the money is still a problem, I sometimes suggest a payment plan. Whether I am willing to make a payment plan with them depends on my current sales and whether I believe them capable of making the payments and responsible enough to follow through. This is a judgment call that you will have to determine on your own. I know that sometimes I want to help people so much I've made payment plans with people who didn't keep them. I've had to write off thousands of dollars in bad debts. I heard Dave Ramsey say that if you are having trouble getting paid, you don't have a collections problem, you have a sales problem. Ouch. Guilty.

If they don't have the money or can't demonstrate a reasonable payment plan, they aren't a qualified buyer. Move on. It will help you avoid the financial stress of being dependent on people paying you who aren't going to pay you.

Note: a lot of sales people believe in qualifying the buyer much sooner in the sales process. I've found it doesn't really fit in with my system, since you are calling to make a friend and/or establish a relationship with someone who may not buy from you herself but might refer a lot of people to you. The moment you introduce cost into the conversation, it is now a sales call. So I don't introduce this until they have clearly indicated an interest in buying my services.

However, if when you're getting acquainted they share with you that business has been terrible and they had to move back in with their mother because they couldn't afford the rent, you can take that as an indication that they probably won't have the money for your product or service. But their mother might, so it's still a possibility!

3. **Too far to drive:** "You're in West LA and I'm in Studio City. I'll never make it there in rush-hour traffic!"

Traffic is tough in the Los Angeles area. Driving time at rush hour is a real concern. I acknowledge the distance is an inconvenience, but then I reinforce the positive benefits: Would it be worth driving the distance for eight weeks if they knew they would have (whatever their hot button financial goal is) at the end of it? I let them know that participants have driven to Brentwood from Long Beach, San Dimas, Palos Verdes, Orange, Camarillo, and even Santa Barbara. One woman flew in from New Mexico each week to attend, and another flew in weekly from Sacramento! But I had a woman in Studio City (about a forty-five-minute drive) that said it was too far to go. In the end, either they want what you have badly enough to do what it takes to get there, or they don't.

9. Ask for the order again!

When you think you have handled their objections and they seem to be more willing to say yes but still can't quite make up their mind, here is a helpful close you might use: the "Benjamin Franklin" close.

This is one of those old sales closes that is very useful in these situations. Tell the customer that there are always arguments for and against buying any product or service. A great way to sort through the pros and cons is to make a list of both. Ask them to draw a vertical line down the center of a piece of paper and label the top "Pro" on the left side and "Con" on the right side. Help them list all the pros first and think of every possible good thing that could result from their purchase of your product or service. You enthusiastically acknowledge all the good things that could happen. Once you have a long list, then say, "Okay, now let's look at the downside. What could be the problem with buying this now?"

Now let them come up with the objections by themselves—you don't have to help them with this part. They have been used to your helping them, and it will be more difficult for them to come up with objections on their own. The result is usually a very short list of objections, like time and money. Now you reaffirm the reasons why they should buy—and there are so many more reasons to say yes than to say no that this very often closes the sale.

Note: Is this technique a bit manipulative? Yes. That's why you have to have integrity about the process. Occasionally I will use a little technique to help someone buy something I *truly believe* will improve their life. And since I offer a money-back guarantee on my program, if for some reason they aren't successful with it, they don't lose anything. That's what makes me comfortable using certain techniques judiciously to sell my workshops. If you believe you can do this with integrity, then use them. If you feel bad or guilty about using any sales technique, you almost certainly will communicate that, and the prospect will pick up on it and their trust in you will disappear.

10. If they're still undecided, let them off the hook.

Sometimes people just aren't ready yet. Timing is important. They think they want it but they're not sure. Or they're scared to try it, afraid they won't use it, it won't work, or they'll have wasted their money. Or it's too soon in the sales process—it's often said that it takes seven to thirteen touches for someone to be ready to buy. That means they need to see you, talk with you on the phone, get a letter, get two emails, get another call, etc. until you've reached twelve interactions.

They may just need more time, like the runny Jell-O needs another hour in the fridge. Don't push it or it will never jell—you'll turn them off and lose them forever. Thank them for the time they've spent with you, acknowledge that they can have time to think about it, and tell them you'll send them some information, put them on your email list, or something. I will say, "Listen, I always fill up my workshops. I don't have to have you there for me to be okay. I just want to make sure you have all the information you need to make the best decision for you." It relaxes people when they think you aren't trying to sell them. Then you can put them on your mailing list, send them some dynamite material including testimonial letters, and follow up with them another day.

11. What if the customer says no?

I have three files for prospects: hot, warm, and dead. Hot prospects are those I expect will buy now, warm prospects I expect will buy later, and dead ones are people who have given me a clear no—they are not interested, can't use it, don't want it. Put them in the dead file and forget it. As marketing expert Gene Call once told me, "Don't waste your time trying to sell lawnmowers to people who live in apartments." You have to work too hard when you do that because first you have to sell them on the idea of moving to a house with a lawn, see? Much too much work.

No has many meanings, from "I don't have enough time to do this" to "I don't want to do this." It may mean that they are too busy, this isn't their priority right now, they're afraid to move forward in this area, they don't believe they can utilize the information properly, they don't have the money, they don't want to spend the money, they're afraid they won't ever be able to have what they want, or they aren't sure what you have will work for them.

It doesn't mean they hate what you do and they hate you.

My friend, Adriane, sells Internet advertising. She makes calls all day long. When people say no to her, she asks, "Is this a 'no' or a 'no-no'?" They always ask what the difference is. She tells them that a "no" is a "not now" and a "no-no" is "not ever." She does this with a smile and a little laugh, and they almost always tell her it's just a "no" and not a "no-no." But if people do tell you it's a "no-no," thank them very much for being honest with you. They are saving you time and energy you can now spend following up with someone who does need or want your services.

12. After the sale, reconfirm.

You need to follow up to reconfirm the sale. Send a confirmation notice, which should also contain your cancellation policy. Call to remind people a week before delivery. You want to keep them involved in the process and excited about the product or service so that they don't get cold feet and cancel. For my teleclasses, I send people a welcome letter, the call-in instructions, and an "intended results" form. When they send the form back to me, I give them feedback about their goals and tell them how excited I am to be working with them and helping them to achieve all their goals. And truly I am!

After delivery of your product or service, call and ask them if everything's okay. Ask them to fill out an evaluation form or "Were you happy with the service?" card. Just doing the sale is not enough—you want to make sure you have a happy, satisfied customer. Customers who are well served become your best salespeople and best advertisers. You want to find out if there is anything they are unhappy about so that you can fix it.

13. Get referrals.

"Who do you know who could also benefit from this product or service?" "Who do you know who…" is a gold mine of a question. The best time for this is after you have delivered the product or service and when you have a delighted customer. They will give you names of people they know who you can now call as a warm call because you have a reference. This is a great way to develop new business.

14. Ask for testimonials and references.

If they are a *really* satisfied customer, ask if they will write you a testimonial letter. Collect a file full of glowing testimonials and send copies of them to prospects. Have a list of satisfied customers with their phone numbers so hesitant buyers can talk to them. That other people have had great success with your product or service is the best selling tool anyone can have. If many others have benefited, your prospect feels more comfortable that he/she will benefit too.

I've worked with so many people after all these years, I almost always have a testimonial from someone with the same concerns or in the same business as the person I'm talking with. When the prospect is skeptical, I tell them about Jess, the auto broker, who told me when he started the class that November and December were traditionally his lowest months for sales. But at the end of the class, these were the two biggest months he ever had. Or if they are in a new business, I'll share about the middle-aged woman who had just started a new career in real estate and hadn't sold a house in eleven months. She sold four homes within two months of the class.

You see? You need to ask all your happy clients for testimonials, save them, and have them ready to share with people who need evidence that you can help them.

15. Cultivate centers of influence.

Who are the movers and shakers in your networking groups, industry, or related fields? You might want to give a reduced rate or even invite them to sample your product or service for free, because if they are delighted with it, they will be in a position to give you testimonials and send you referrals. That's why the celebrities on the red carpet get to wear million-dollar Harry Winston jewels for free.

Carol Schafer, owner of Mink N More Jewelry, was new to one of my networking groups and wanted to get known in the group fast. As I was admiring her jewelry at a meeting, it suddenly struck me that our fancy-dress awards banquet was coming up, and she could copy Harry Winston and have all the award nominees wear her jewelry! She was delighted with the idea and let me wear a gorgeous necklace too. All night long, I told every person I talked to that "I am wearing Carol Schafer this evening." It was such a kick! We had fun, Carol got better known in the organization, and I know she sold some jewelry—I bought some!

Cultivating influential people is an especially good thing to do if you are new at your business or new to a particular networking group. Find the most prominent person you can and get to know them, send them a referral, buy their product or service—something that will get you into their circle of influence.

16. Learn how to handle cancellations and do resales.

It sometimes happens that customers experience that terrible affliction—cold feet or buyer's remorse. Most of the time, this happens at the last minute, right before the delivery of the product or service. Now, after the sale, you have to do the resale.

This is where the notes that you took during the original conversation about what the customer wanted and needed come in handy. You have to reinforce all the positive benefits and overcome all the objections all over again. You must not appear to be needy or concerned for yourself but concerned for them and the wisdom of their choice. Take them back over all their wants and needs. Sometimes it's an unavoidable event that pushes the sale back in time—it's not lost, just postponed. But if you sense that it is one of the objections come back to haunt you, take them through the benefits of buying again. As a last resort, remind them of your cancellation policy if they are calling past the time where they are due a refund.

17. Follow up—call, call, recall, and call again.

Several years ago, I read a study in which the top national salespeople were asked how many times they had to ask a customer for the order. The national average for the very top salespeople was—*six!* Not only that, but 65 percent of the salespeople *never* asked for the order. So don't feel badly if you've asked three times and gotten "Maybe," "I'll think about it," "Later," "Sometime," and "I'll have to ask my husband" all three times. Don't give up! Persistence pays off. You have to start all over again at step one and find more rapport or have a conversation about other things before getting around to your product or service again. Then go through all the steps again and ask for the order again. Repeat as necessary. Keep asking until they say yes or give you a clear no.

When I started a daily blog using material from my books and writing new posts, I received a note from a Facebook friend who said, "I always thought you were cool and loved hearing you speak at networking events and women's conferences. But now I am simply in awe. I signed up for your daily affirmations. I can't tell you how much I love them. I sent a copy to my boyfriend and he said, 'When can we take her workshop?'"

As you know by now, that question is a big buying signal! This was someone I should definitely follow up with to explore the possibilities of them taking the next class. So I wrote her back and said we should talk. But I didn't hear back from her during the next week.

And this is where a lot of people lose their sale. They don't follow up *again*. Remember, it takes seven to thirteen touches before someone is ready to buy from you, but even when they are leaning toward yes, you have to close the deal.

So I did a Google search and found the woman's website with her phone number. I called her up, we had a lovely chat, and she enrolled in the course. I asked about her boyfriend, and she said she would talk with him. Then she wrote, "I just want you to know that I hung up the phone with you and immediately downloaded your books to my Nook. Yay." A few hours after that, she wrote me to say her boyfriend was in too.

My advertising and the blog were working, driving traffic to my website, helping to let the world know I had books and workshops. But the sale doesn't magically happen by itself. It needs a little assist. The advertising is in the blog. The money is in the phone!

18. Repeat the above with the next prospect!

This telephone sales script works best for higher ticket sales. This doesn't work if you're selling ten-dollar items. You can't have one-on-one telephone conversations for an hour if you're only making ten dollars. If you're selling small-ticket items, you have to have conversations with buyers that buy in bulk, like the buyer for Target or Nordstrom or Amazon. Or, like network marketers, you focus on people who will sell multiple quantities for you. You will have to figure out what works best for you in your particular business. But the above sales model works great for sole practitioners, home-based business owners, independent contractors, freelancers, and network marketers of all kinds.

It works if you work it! Pick up the golden phone and send out some ships to bring in your treasure.

Growth Happens Outside Your Comfort Zone

"Perseverance is a great element of success. If you only knock long enough and loud enough at the gate, you are sure to wake up somebody."
—Henry Wadsworth Longfellow

Remember Dorothy in *The Wizard of Oz* knocking on the door of the Emerald City, begging to be allowed in? She was in a strange land among strangers, and every step she took was outside her comfort zone. When you're Dorothy and your goal is to get home, you are willing to take any path to get there. Your goal is all that matters.

This is what it takes to be successful at anything: passion, determination, and single-minded devotion to purpose. Determination is like an iron fist holding up your spine. If the Emerald City holds the map to your way home, you will not be dissuaded from your dream because there's a wicked witch on the road or flying monkeys overhead or a guard at the gate who denies you entrance. You will never be one of those small people who are content to stay forever in Munchkinland. You will get to the Emerald City or die on the road. And because you keep on moving down the road, life helps you out by sending you a Glinda, a Tin Man, a Scarecrow, and a Cowardly Lion to give you encouragement and help you succeed.

Losing fires up winners. Their response when someone tells them they aren't good enough, they can't do it, or they're a loser is "Oh, yeah? Watch this!" They use the rejection as an energetic launching pad to redouble their efforts, sharpen their creativity, and prove the naysayers wrong.

Let me give you a tip: there's no "there" there. There is no place to get to where you stay put "happily ever after." Because after you reach your Emerald City, it isn't long before you're making plans for the Ruby City next. And the Diamond City after that. As soon as you get one goal, you just set another goal. Goals are not ends in themselves— they are just there to get you out on the road, meeting people and experiencing life. Be passionate and follow your bliss, and the worst that can happen is you live a life full of great adventures. Enjoy it all!

Risk

One afternoon, someone posted a cartoon on Facebook. In the bottom left-hand corner was a little fluffy cloud that was labeled "your comfort zone." In the upper right-hand corner, there was a huge cloud that was labeled "where the magic happens."

If we're ever going to reach any of our goals, we have to learn to get comfortable being uncomfortable. We're never comfortable doing new things, going new places, or meeting new people. It's an adventure and a mystery—we don't know what will happen, whether we will be admired, accepted, and loved or rejected, dismissed, and disliked. We're much more comfortable being with people where we already know we are accepted and liked. We like situations that we've been in before so we know what to expect and that we can handle it.

But if you always do what you've always done, you'll always get what you've always gotten, as the saying goes. If what you're getting now is perfect for you, by all means, keep on doing it. But do a few unexpected things now and then too, or you may miss out on some of the most wonderful people and glorious experiences of your life! Yes, it could be worse…but it could be so much better too! How will you know if you don't try out some new things?

Here are a few suggestions to get your creative juices flowing:

- Go to a networking group you've never attended before.
- Reach out to someone on Facebook or some other social media site.
- Begin a conversation with a stranger.
- Open up to let something new and wonderful into your life.
- Have an adventure, and share about it. You may help others have the courage to step into adventures too.

I've read reports that said people are twice as fearful of losing money as they are hopeful of gaining money. That means most people hang on to money out of fear when they should be investing money in things that will pay off. Holding on to money doesn't produce any more money, does it?

There is no success without risk.

Paul McCartney's Risk

"One day John and George showed up…and told me we had a gig… I said, 'No. I've got a steady job here… I can't expect more.' And I was quite serious… But then…I thought, 'Sod it…' I bunked over the wall and was never seen again by Massey and Coggins. Pretty shrewd move really, as things turned out."

—Sir Paul McCartney, *The Beatles Anthology*

It seems ridiculous now that Paul McCartney would ever have thought he should just stay in his safe nine-to-five job. But I wonder how many people, when faced with the same decision, stick with the secure job and don't ever try to achieve their dreams? Do you know someone who could have been a professional ball player but never tried out for the team? Or a dancer who was too afraid to audition for the American Ballet Theatre? Maybe a friend of yours could sew up a storm but couldn't see that she could be a fashion designer.

When I decided to go full-time in the workshop business and leave bookkeeping behind, I didn't know if I could make it work as a business. I just knew I loved it and had to try. And here I am, more than twenty years later, and I'm still loving it, still enrolling people, still thrilled with mentoring and teaching people, still making money. Yes! It works.

Oh, I can also still look ahead to the workshop after this one and cry, "Oh no, there's nobody in my next workshop! What if I've already gotten everyone who's gettable? What if the competition gets them before I do? What if…"

You can play the "what if" game too, can't you? But it won't do you or anyone else any good. I saw this quote by Louise L. Hay recently: "I do not fix problems. I fix my thinking. Then problems fix themselves."

A photographer client of mine once made me absolutely crazy with his "what ifs." It was like he was determined to be anxious. As we worked together in class, he had clients and photography assignments lined up four months in advance, and then six months, and then nine months! But it didn't matter how far ahead he was guaranteed work—he could always see ahead to that blank space in the future where the unknown lurked. And what would he do then?

How much of a guarantee would make him feel safe? One year?

Five years? That's a zero-sum game. Look, you can't even know that you'll be *alive* nine months from now or even *tomorrow*. So give up the worries and spend all your creative energy on figuring out how to make money serving others and doing what you want. That's how you'll enrich the world as well as yourself.

The only reasonable "what if" is this one: What if Paul McCartney had continued to work at Massey and Coggins?

Are You an Artist?

It's been said that if you ask kindergartners if they are artists, 100 percent of them say yes.

But if you ask fifth graders if they're artists, only 10 percent say yes.

Isn't that sad? Somehow between the ages of five and ten, children get the message—from school, their parents, their friends, their peers, the media—that they aren't artists or that they aren't creative.

But we are all artists and are creative all the time, with every choice we make, every item of decoration, clothing, makeup, jewelry, furniture, housing, or transportation we pick. Stop the judgments; stop comparing yourself to someone else's choice of style or color. Yes, you can appreciate another person's flair or creativity, but the point is not to put yourself down with it but to be inspired by it. Let your own creative soul express itself and soar.

Start taking little risks. Buy an article of clothing that's just a little outside your comfort zone—a wild color that doesn't go with anything else or a funky piece of jewelry that isn't your usual style. Go to a sci-fi movie if you never do, or go see a children's cartoon even if you don't have children. Reach out and make a phone call to someone you might not ordinarily call.

Break the chains of habit and circumspection and create your life anew just a little bit today. You are an artist, and your canvas is your life.

Allow the Spirit of Creativity to Take Over

There are certain stories I wrote in *The Wealthy Spirit* that I absolutely love. I can say that with modesty, even though I wrote them, because I'm not sure how I wrote them. They are evidence of the magical things that happen when you are "in the zone." They just came through as I sat at my computer typing and thinking and writing. Once in a while, something else took hold, the zone embraced me, and images flowed through my mind and became words. And the stories flowed from them.

Every artist experiences this otherworldly phenomenon that transforms their picture or article or ad or whatever creation they are working on. This is why we show up hour after hour, day after day. We wait for the inspiration, the muse, the automatic writing that takes over and uses us as a tool. The thing we intended has been transformed and blessed.

This only happens when you are working, experimenting, listening, and giving yourself over to the thing you love. You must make time for this.

Ask for what you want today. Then give yourself over to it, expecting the best. Transformation awaits you.

If you put your neck out and try, you've got a fifty-fifty shot of being successful. If you don't try, you've got a zero shot at being successful. So what would you rather have? A 50 percent chance of success or a 0 percent chance?

Part of this comes from the actor's credo that you always say "Yes!" on an audition when they ask you "Can you (fill in the blank)?" Of course, if it turned out to be skydiving or something else that you couldn't fake, you could always back up and say so afterward. I'm not pretending I can do anything where the downside is death.

Back in my acting days, I was cast in a musical at Walt Disney World called *Show Me America!* Larry Billman, the director of the musical, told me the story of casting actress Teri Garr in a major role in the show when it was originated at Disneyland two years before. She was to play the Statue of Liberty, who was the narrator of the show, and do it on roller skates. Teri wrote about this incident in her book *Speedbumps: Flooring It Through Hollywood,* but here's my recollection of how Larry shared it with me.

At the audition, Larry asked her if she could roller skate. "Oh, yes," Teri exclaimed. "I love roller skating. I roller skate all the time. I was practically a professional roller skater!"

She was cast in the show and was terrifically funny in the part. She did a great job all through rehearsals, but finally the day came for dress rehearsal, and she had to do it on roller skates.

She couldn't skate at all. She lurched, waved her arms madly, then sailed across the stage until she ran into something that stopped her. Sometimes she just continued rolling right off into the wings where someone would grab her, turn her around, and push her back onstage.

She must have been afraid she was going to be fired. But Larry was laughing helplessly, with tears rolling down his face.

"You've never been on skates before, have you?" he accused.

"Only when I was a kid," she admitted sheepishly.

"Well, lucky for you, you are screamingly funny not being able to skate, so we're leaving you in," Larry told her. She fell into the orchestra pit at least once a week, shouting, "Lookout, John, here I come!" to the conductor.

Throughout the run of the show, audiences howled with laughter at her brilliant performance. If Teri had told Larry at the audition that she couldn't skate, she probably wouldn't have gotten the part.

After writing this story, I found Larry on Facebook and sent it to him. He commented, "Chutzpah is the secret to get doors 'opened.' But once inside you have to deliver the goods as you did. Thanks for sharing this story… I still see her as often as possible. I have such admiration for that adorable, nonskating comedienne who became the inspiration she is now in her medical challenges. Now, THAT'S chutzpah."

Larry was so right. In 2002, Teri Garr disclosed that she was battling multiple sclerosis (MS). Wikipedia reports, "After disclosing her condition, she became a National Ambassador for the National Multiple Sclerosis Society and National Chair for the Society's Women Against MS program (WAMS). In November 2005, Garr was honored as the society's Ambassador of the Year. This honor had been given only four times since the society was founded."

So let Teri be a role model for you. Have a little chutzpah already. Say yes and wing it!

"Yeah, But…"

I warn people in my coaching practice to beware of this phrase. It's usually followed by an objection: "Yeah, but I can't because my business is different" or "Yeah, but I tried that once in 1995 and it didn't work" or "Yeah, but I'm not good at that."

I admit to being a world-class yeah-butter myself.

Surprised?

Yes. We often teach best what we need to learn most, as Richard Bach said in *Illusions*.

When someone said, "Chellie, you should teach workshops!" I said, "Yeah, but I don't think I can do that."

When someone said, "Chellie, you should write a book!" I said, "Yeah, but that's too much work and I don't want to schlep product around."

When someone said, "Chellie, you should franchise your workshops!" I said, "Yeah, but I'm not ready to do that yet."

Upon reflection, I think "yeah, buts" are often the way we work things out in our minds before we take action. We do need to be thankful for the cautionary voice inside us that reminds us that there might be potential downsides to our plan. We have to consider the ramifications of our actions before embarking on a new course of action. What are the problems we might encounter? What would we be willing to do to surmount them? How might our life be changed if we get what we want?

And then we have to be prepared with a plan B if plan A doesn't pan out…

Sometimes "yeah, but" is just a wishy-washy way of saying we don't want to do it. So pause the next time you're about to say "yeah, but" and think if what you really mean is "Thanks for the suggestion, but I've decided against doing that." It's certainly fine to say no.

But you want to be careful not to shut down your creative contributors from having great ideas for you. You want them to keep coming, because sometimes they have an idea that is so perfect for you, your answer is going to be, "Wow! That's a fabulous idea! I'm going to get started on that right away!"

Isn't that what you most want to hear when you offer someone a suggestion?

The Audition I Almost Skipped

Back in my acting days, I got a call to audition for a Pillsbury flour television commercial. They were looking for my "type"—a young female homemaker baking in the kitchen. But it was going to be a regional commercial that would run in the southern United States, so they stressed that an authentic Southern accent was required.

I called my boyfriend Stan about the casting opportunity but told him I didn't think it was right for me because I wasn't really from the South. I knew what they wanted because my mother was born and raised in Mississippi, and although she had lived in California for twenty-five years, she never lost her accent.

"Chellie, have you ever listened to yourself after you talk with your mother?" Stan admonished me. "Just call your mom and talk with her for five minutes before the audition. You'll be fine!"

I had to laugh at that, so I invented an affirmation for myself that I spoke with a perfect Southern accent. Then I followed his instructions and had a lovely talk with my mom, and sure enough, her lilting drawl started creeping into my speech pattern.

When the producers and director called me into the casting area and had me stand in front of the camera, the director said amiably, "Hi, Chellie."

"Hi, y'all," I replied. (Phonetically, this sounds like "Haa, yawl.")

He grinned and said, "Chellie is an interesting name. Where did that come from?"

"It's a family name," I drawled. "My mother is from Mississippi and her name is Chellie LeNell. My grandmother is Chellie Estelle, my cousin is Chellie Lou, and I'm Chellie Lynn."

Everyone in the room perked up and laughed at that.

"Isn't that confusing at family reunions?" he asked.

"No, sir. It's the South, you know, and we always use two names, like Billy Jo and Jim Bob, and so there's no mistake at all."

I got the job.

Have you ever talked your way into believing in something that on the face of it looked like it couldn't happen—but then you did it anyway? Go for your dream today, no matter what "facts" are standing in your way!

Some of Your Decisions Are Going to Be Bad Decisions

In the documentary *History of the Eagles: The Story of an American Band*, Glenn Frey reported that Pete Seeger told him that he needed to write songs.

"But what if they're bad?" he asked.

"They're going to be bad," Pete answered. "That's okay. Just keep writing songs and eventually you'll write a good song."

So Glenn started writing songs. They weren't very good and he was frustrated. But then he said he moved into a very small apartment in Los Angeles, and Jackson Browne lived in the basement below him. He would listen to Jackson play a musical phrase on the piano, over and over and over. Then there would be a long pause. Then Jackson would play the phrase again, along with another phrase, over and over and over. Then silence. Then he'd play the phrase again, with a change. Over and over and over.

Glenn said that's what taught him how to go about writing songs—it's work! My friend Zeda Speigel and I were talking about that one day and she agreed. "That's why I never took ballet lessons," she said. "I just wasn't willing to be bad at it for as long as it would take to get good at it."

You have to love your goal enough to suffer through the bad patches. You're going to write bad songs. You're going to make bad sales calls. You're going to make mistakes giving a speech. You're going to ask for a promotion and not get it.

So what?

After you do it wrong, figure out where the mistake was and practice the correction. You can't figure out everything ahead of time so perfectly that you avoid ever making mistakes. Being willing to be wrong, to make mistakes, and to look foolish is another lesson I learned from acting. Acting teachers always stress that you have to release your inhibitions and experiment—that you have to be willing to look foolish if you're ever going to find the truth of a moment. That spontaneity is what leads to great acting.

It can be useful to think about different future scenarios, looking to see what is the best course of action. It helps to bounce ideas off someone else and see what they think. Brainstorming with a select group of trusted advisers is a very illuminating process. Then it must be followed by positive action in the chosen direction. After you do it, you'll figure out whether it was right or not, and then you can correct it for the next time.

Ready, fire, aim! Fire again!

There is no way to know beforehand if what you are going to try will produce the result you want. You can endlessly search for the perfect consultant, you can doubt every person you hire, and you can always think of someone else who might have been better. But this kind of second-guessing just steals your energy and projects fear of failure into your visions of the future. At some point, you just have to make a decision to the best of your ability in the moment. Then stick with it.

Have faith in your choice until you're given a reason not to. Then you can choose again.

When It Doesn't Work Out

We all get trapped in our limited perspectives and need a friend to give us a metaphorical kick in the rear from time to time.

One of my dear friends still remembers the day she changed the direction of her life. She had called me to talk because she was drawn to the idea of becoming a psychotherapist. But it was going to take years of study and then internship, and she was agonizing over what she was going to have to give up to do it.

"How can I give up my acting career after all these years?" she wailed.

As gently as I could, I said, "What career?"

There was silence on the phone, and then… "Ah."

She really hadn't been doing any acting except in community theater or showcase productions—all things that didn't pay. She knew that, but all the activity kept the illusion of success alive, even though there wasn't an income to back it up.

I thought that she would make a fabulous therapist. She had always been such a supportive friend, with brilliant ideas, wonderful enthusiasm, and kick-ass advice. I wanted to see her achieve the success she dreamed of, even if the vehicle that brought her satisfaction was a different career than the one she had imagined.

Old dreams die hard—especially when you've learned to have persistence and keep trying even in the face of impossible odds and insurmountable obstacles. You don't want to let go of the dream because maybe today you'll be discovered, your ship will come in and Oprah will call, the publisher will say yes, or the starring role will be offered. You dream until one day your dreams come true, or one day you wake up and discover your dream has changed.

That's what happened to me when I discovered I loved a bookkeeping job more than I loved acting. I could never have predicted that would happen! You change directions when what once brought you joy doesn't any longer, and you look for another way to get it. A friend helped me make that shift when she identified the real success I was after that could be found in any profession: good friends, good work, good praise, and good money.

My friend enrolled in psychology courses, got her license in marriage and family therapy (LMFT), did her internship, and has been happily running a successful private practice helping people for many years. And on the side, she still acts in community theater and has a ball. And that's success too.

The Spider at the Gate

How do we know if we need to change careers or find a different business to be successful, or if it's the things we're doing? Is it the business that's at fault or the business plan?

I learned this lesson from a spider.

Each night, the little spider at my front gate works busily, weaving his web to catch his morning breakfast. He is diligent and hard-working, he studied design and construction, and he makes a fine web.

But every morning, I break his web apart as I pass through to collect my morning newspaper. I'm sure the spider sees the destruction and whines, "Why does this always happen to me? I work as hard as any other spider I know. I'm so unlucky! It's not fair!"

The spider at my gate isn't unlucky—he has just chosen the wrong location for his business. Apparently, he didn't have the advice of a good real estate agent who could have told him the three most important rules: location, location, location!

Other spiders choose the right real estate, but then just sit there and chant, "I'm catching lots of flies, I'm catching lots of flies..." But they don't build a web to catch them, so all the flies just zoom on by. Then they complain, "Those silly affirmations never work!"

Like spiders, we all have blind spots that keep us from attaining our goals, having all the clients we want, and making all the money we desire. We need teachers, mentors, and trainers to help us see the holes in our programs, devise the remedies to fix them, and practice our new choices until they become our new habits.

We know we need to learn, but we resist. "It costs too much!" we complain. "It takes too long!" "I'm too overwhelmed." "It's too far to drive." "I have small children." "My parents need help..." And we sit by our webs in the wrong location or chant affirmations without any web and wonder why we don't have any money or why our dreams haven't come true.

Get into a workshop! Sign up for a class! Hire a coach, join a mastermind group, get into therapy. Buy books on sales, marketing, self-esteem, metaphysics, personal empowerment. Take some action to learn something new so you can get new results. Help is all around you—reach out and take it! Invest your time, invest your money, and you will reap the rewards you crave. You invested time and money in learning the skills of your profession, didn't you? You didn't make it up from scratch. So invest some time and money in learning how to apply them so that your business is successful or you get the promotion you desire. You deserve it!

Dream Big—Nothing Is Impossible

How big is the dream you have? Who's to say it's impossible?

For most of recorded history, people had lists of things that were impossible—flight, space flight, talking long distance, seeing long distance, replacing limbs or organs. Bit by bit and byte by byte, we've done all of these things. Nothing seems impossible anymore—we just acknowledge that we haven't invented the technology yet.

My dad was an aerospace engineer, and I grew up watching all the rocket liftoffs at 5:00 a.m. with the family. I loved reading his science fiction magazines and novels, which spoke of space flight to other worlds, robots to do our bidding, and new technological inventions like virtual reality or handheld computers.

Science fiction authors invented many things in common use today. Jules Verne foresaw scuba diving in 1870, Edward Bellamy wrote about credit cards in 1888, and H. G. Wells described a flat surface with moving pictures in 1899, which we now know as a tablet computer. Mark Twain wrote about a global communication device like the Internet in 1904, genetic engineering was introduced by Aldous Huxley in 1931, and satellites were mentioned by Isaac Asimov in 1945.

I remember watching *Star Trek* and all the kids thought how cool it was that they had "communicators" they could flip open to talk to one another. Now, cell phones are everyday reality. They had to take out the House of Tomorrow at Disneyland when everything in it became widely used in everyday life. Science fiction becomes science fact on a regular basis. If you can believe it, you can achieve it.

There weren't very many good science fiction films when I was growing up—*Forbidden Planet* was the best of the lot. There was only one woman in the entire movie, which was fairly typical of the genre. Although it was still largely a male universe, sci-fi films radically improved in the '70s with the advent of *Star Wars.*

I saw it on opening day at the Chinese Theater in Hollywood with my dear actress friend, Gaye Kruger, and an actor friend of hers named Ty. I'll never forget it. When the space ships flew overhead in the very beginning of the movie, the audience roared and cheered and continued clapping for the entire opening battle sequence. We were electrified by the story, the special effects, everything. It was a wonderful group experience; the audience was enthralled as one being and gave the film a standing ovation. (There is an energy to watching a movie as a group that is entirely missing from watching a movie alone. Don't you feel that?)

After the movie, the three of us went back to Gaye's apartment, where we called Mark Hamill, who played the young hero, Luke Skywalker. Gaye knew him from a film project and I had met him before on several commercial auditions. When I grabbed the phone, I just raved about the movie and his part in it. I remember he was so tickled we liked it and kept saying, "Really? You really liked it? I'm so glad!"

Of course, this was way before it took off—no one knew that this little film was going to be a huge juggernaut and the highest grossing film of all time (well, until 1982 with *E.T., the Extra-Terrestrial*). It also started a wave of science and speculative fiction movies and television I've enjoyed ever since.

I'm also grateful that there are more women in the sci-fi movies now. The reinvention of *Battlestar Galactica* by Ronald D. Moore in 2004 starred many women in traditionally male roles—even the most adventurous fighter pilot, Starbuck, was recast as a woman. Jennifer Lawrence of *The Hunger Games* movies proved that a woman could star in a science fiction action-adventure and gross over $150 million opening weekend. Progress!

"To boldly go where no one has gone before." That's what all creative artists do. No matter what cost or outcome. I thank God and my lucky stars for all the people who follow their dreams and create this rich life I enjoy. I'm grateful for all those who turn their dreams into reality and invent personal computers, eyeglasses, microwave ovens, washing machines, and televisions. My dad said the real miracle of landing a man on the moon was that we all watched him land on the moon on television.

Audrey Hepburn said, "Nothing is impossible, the word itself says 'I'm possible'!" What do you want to invent? What star are you following? Let your creativity expand your reality. Go. Boldly!

Change Exercise

I give this exercise in my workshop—to make some little changes. Simple ones like part your hair on the other side (feels really weird), put your other shoe on first (didn't know you did it the same every day, did you?), or change the way you put the toilet paper on the toilet paper holder (if you always have it going over the top, put it so the paper comes out underneath).

Truly compulsive behavior is changing the toilet paper in other people's homes (and yes, I've done that). I saw a funny T-shirt in a catalog that you might relate to too: "I have OCD and ADD— which means I have to be perfect, but not for very long."

It took me a while to figure out that there were some people in class who had no trouble changing things up. They didn't have many routines at all and never did things the same way twice. So the exercise never made them feel awkward or out of sync.

When I figured that out, after giving the exercise instructions, I asked if anyone found that an easy exercise because they were always changing things. Several people smiled and nodded, exclaiming that they never did the same thing.

"Well, don't feel so smug," I said, "because you're going to do the opposite exercise. I want you to invent a routine of seven or eight steps and do that same routine every morning without any changes."

"Oh no!" They moaned and groaned and complained, just like the others who had to mix it up.

Once, a man who was very ordered and compulsive went home and changed all the toilet paper rolls in his home and at work. It drove him crazy every day, and when he came to class, he reported how it upset him to have his routine broken that way.

His wife, who was one of the creative never-do-it-the-same-way-twice types, looked at him in amazement and said, "Honey, I didn't know you did that!"

I tell people then that if they can't change a little thing like the toilet paper, how are they going to change a big thing like their money? Take a look at what you are resistant to changing, and also where you never make a decision about the best way to do something. Both the ability to change and the ability to set a routine are important to establishing a good relationship with money. You need some structure, and some flexibility.

Where do you get stuck? In the structure or in the changes?

Some Changes Sneak Up on You

Wonderful things happen if you just open up your mind to new opportunities and other ways of being. We get so wrapped up in what's "normal" that we think there's something wrong with us if we want to do things differently. But that just may be your higher self calling, whispering in the night that you might like life more if you lived it a little more broadly or deeply, more laughingly or extravagantly.

Years ago, I had an unfortunate experience with my bookkeeping service when our biggest client, who represented 75 percent of my income, left with two weeks' notice. It was a big disaster! I ended up losing my home and my money but kept the business, although it was much smaller. When a friend asked where I was going to live, I said I had no idea. She looked over at our mutual friend, Shelley, who said, "You could live with me."

Her home was gorgeous, two stories, autumn colors, lovely furniture, beautiful art on the walls, and I thought it would be a great place for six months or a year while I got myself (and my money) back together…

My fortunes rose again better than ever after that, but I still live in this house with Shelley. It's been over twenty years now. We're great friends and we both think it's wonderful to share space. An article by Sarah Mahoney in the AARP magazine highlighted that many divorced or widowed women are saving money and gaining companionship by sharing space. "These days more and more women are living two, three, and sometimes more to a house. And they're agreeing on everything from how to split the electric bill to who gets use of the kitchen on Saturday night. Indeed, what was originally thought to be an impossible situation is turning out to be a godsend for many women," she says.

A networking friend of mine saw me at a meeting and said, "You're doing so well now, you can buy your own house!"

I looked at her like she was crazy. "Why would I want to do that?" I asked. "I go buy another house and then Shelley and I both have to live alone or go search for another congenial roommate."

"But it's a good investment," she insisted. (Obviously, this was before the latest financial fiasco.)

"There are plenty of other good investments," I said, "but a great roommate is hard to find!"

A couple of female friends who took my class together decided they loved our idea. They bought a duplex together—one lives upstairs and the other downstairs. Terrific!

Some people are unhappy because they aren't living the American dream. Many more are unhappy because they're living it and it doesn't suit them. I'm living my own version of the Chellie dream, the one I created outside the usual box.

How do you create your dream life? Reexamine everything you

were ever taught was the right thing to do. Take another look at what you were told you should never do. Sometimes you have to ignore conventional advice because although it might be perfect for most people, it might not work for you. Start from scratch. Put everything in your dream that makes you happy, and leave out everything that makes you stressed.

Learn to Say No to Protect Your Boundaries

My friend and author of *Fearless Living*, Rhonda Britten, says, "If you don't have a *no*, your *yes* means nothing."

That really resonated with me, as it was often so hard for me to say no. Whenever anyone asked for help, I said yes. If people wanted me to volunteer for a board, I said yes. I was constantly overwhelmed, having signed up for too many things, rushing around to try to get everything done.

In my senior year of high school, I was the lead in the school play, worthy adviser of Rainbow Girls, and pep chairman all at the same time. One semester in college, I was in a semiprofessional dance company, choreographing and playing a part in the college production, and rehearsed a reader's theater piece from midnight to 4:00 a.m. because that was the only time I was available! Oh yes, and carried nineteen units in school too. It was all engaging and interesting and I loved all of it, but it would have been much better if it had not all happened at the same time! I practically had a nervous breakdown from the stress. Somewhere in my psyche, I knew I was nuts.

When I read *When I Say No, I Feel Guilty* by Manuel Smith, I started to understand how to unwind from so many duties and responsibilities. I could just smile and say, "Thank you so much for asking me and I'd love to, but unfortunately I have a full slate of commitments right now and can't take that on. Good luck with your project, and let me know how it goes!"

One time some friends in a networking group suggested I run for president of the club. I smiled and said, "Thank you so much for asking me and I'd love to, but…"

One man said, "But, Chellie, you'd make a great president!"

I said, "Thank you very much. I appreciate your confidence in me, but no."

"Why not?" he pressed.

"Because I've been president of every club I've belonged to since I was twelve," I replied with a twinkle in my eye. "Time for somebody else to have a crack at it!"

If you're too rushed, you won't be happy. You need time to rest, reflect, and enjoy your activities. Make a list of everything you're doing in order of priority, then chop off the bottom third and resign, quit, abdicate, or withdraw from them.

You might find a golden treasure at the end of that rainbow: free time.

Another Reason to Say No— Wrong Job, Bad Boss, Bad Clients

Back in the '80s, I worked for Edgar Scherick and Scott Rudin, who was rather the "boy wonder" in his early twenties then. He has since come a very long way up to the top of the Hollywood food chain. Producer of many top-of-the-line films including *The Hours*, *The Addams Family*, *The Queen*, and more recently *The Social Network*, he has won many honors, including the Academy Award for Best Picture for *No Country for Old Men*.

He was also awarded the dubious title of one of "New York's Worst Bosses" on Gawker.com in 2007 and was profiled in a *Wall Street Journal* article entitled "Boss-Zilla." Shudder. One account mentions he once went through 250 assistants in one year (although he claimed he could only count 119). He was reputed to be the model for the evil producer played by Kevin Spacey in *Swimming with Sharks.* (I wrote a story in *The Wealthy Spirit* about telling Scott no, that I wouldn't run an errand for him. A reader sent me a note saying, "Chellie, you badass! You said no to Scott Rudin. That must be on the bucket list of thousands of assistants.")

Oh, dear. He wasn't quite that bad when I worked for him— I'm sure it was fortunate for me that he was in New York most of the time. Actually, I liked and admired him—he was brilliant and creative and quick, and we got along.

Edgar was the scary one to me. Unlike Scott, he was there every day. He would scream at the top of his lungs and turn red in the face. Once he yelled at a production assistant who hadn't accomplished a task, jumped up on my desk, and pounded the ceiling until plaster rained down on the three of us!

Picture me as a small animal that freezes in place because motion attracts the predator. When he jumped off the table and looked at me, I just said, "So do you want to call Freddie Fields now?" They told me later he said I was "unflappable." Nope, frozen stiff is what I was, but redirection was a tool I found handy for survival.

I had taken the job with Scott because I wanted to be a producer's assistant. I figured I would get an overview of all the jobs in the film industry and then I could decide if there was a job I wanted to do on the other side of the camera. But the two years I spent with Scott and Edgar convinced me that it was no place for me. There was just too much yelling. I felt I'd have to become used to that or become a screamer myself, and I just didn't have it in me to do either. I remember the day I opened up the want ads and prayed, "Please, God, please—help me find a nice little bookkeeping job again with nice, normal people."

And soon enough, off I went. Pretty good move too, as it turned out. It was there that I developed my Financial Stress Reduction workshops. I love my life!

And there's no yelling.

Tell the Truth about Yourself— No Matter Who Likes It (or Doesn't)

I've always considered myself a little bit "left of center," but for most of my life, I just tried hard to fit in, do what was expected, do it as well as I could, dress to match the styles others thought best, and make my way in the world following the rules. I was brought up with the phrase "What will the neighbors think?" whenever I strayed from the beaten path.

It took me years to figure out that if I blended in too perfectly, I became invisible. I felt like wallpaper where nothing stands out. I started to become aware that if it seems everybody likes you, you're probably faking it on some level, never letting your true personality shine through. If you go along with the crowd too much of the time, without the crowd you don't know who you are.

Mae West said, "I used to be Snow White, but I drifted."

So let yourself drift. Figure out what you like about yourself that's a little unusual, unique, funny, raunchy, strong, sexy, smart, or weird. Let your edges show. Stop blending in and set your own style.

What will the neighbors think? Some won't like it at all—they'll be threatened or try to squelch you back down into the box. But some will love it and want to get closer and find out more about you. Deep friendships come with that, and freedom.

Years ago, I was standing in line at a wedding reception, and next to me was an old friend from Sunday school. We were reminiscing, and Linda kept mentioning different people from the in-crowd (that I wasn't in) and going on about what they were doing now. The food line was long, I was hungry, and when she finally mentioned yet another girl, I decided a little truth might spice up this conversation.

"I have to tell you, I never liked Jenny," I said. "And I don't care what she's doing now."

Linda's mouth dropped open, and she looked at me wide-eyed

and stopped dead in her tracks. Then she smiled and said with a twinkle, "You know, I never liked her either!"

We both broke into peals of laughter, hugged each other, and then started a real conversation about what we really liked and didn't like. It was fabulous! Instead of party chitchat that we would have forgotten by the time we got in our cars, we discovered a true friendship.

Sow some wild seeds today—you never know what might grow from them!

St. Chellie or ?

I wrote a story in *The Wealthy Spirit* about St. Chellie in my mind. I remember all the times I felt badly about myself and struggled to measure up to the perfect ideal I felt I ought to be. But who can ever look good when held up against perfection?

I look back with some pity on the self-that-was who needed help because I really didn't think I was enough.

I am better now. No, not a better person, just more recovered from the shame of not being a better person, if you take my meaning. At present, I'm quite pleased with myself for the most part.

This is one of the fringe benefits of growing older. If you survive your youth, you find yourself morphing into your strong and wise place. And you get pretty proud of having arrived there too. Self-satisfied and asking for the world to deliver goodies.

I call it my arrogant bitch phase of life.

The Advantage of Going for It Is That Sometimes You Get It!

Alecia Caine reinvented herself several times, having had her own accounting practice and now owning and operating the tour company Find Yourself in France. She started writing a book called *My Paris Story: Living, Loving, and Leaping without a Net in the City of Light* and planned to have the launch party in Paris.

She wrote to tell me how it all happened:

I got my analytical, logical mind from my dad and I learned to be practical and pragmatic. All those coaches who say "just think it and it will come" never worked for my brain. I need action, not just thought, to believe in. One tool I learned from you is to create two or three budgets, the "barely cutting it" budget and the dream budget.

Every week I would prepare my cash-flow projections. I call it the "peace of mind" schedule to see the sources and uses of money in the next weeks. If I needed to manifest money for something, it would first go on the peace of mind schedule. As soon as I did that, the money or the opportunities would show up and I had the clarity I needed to take action. Clarity being the key.

Eventually my faith and trust grew in this process and I started to go from bare minimum to thrive. I started to ask for what I want on my spreadsheet and I made it happen. Now I'm manifesting a dream to live part-time in France. Remember a year ago when I posted I was going to Paris and had to go put it all on a credit card! I went, had a blast, and the money quickly followed.

Another thing I've learned is if you wait to live your life until you have enough money or whatever (fill in the blank), it won't come and you'll always be waiting. Acting "as if" is something I did when I was afraid to do something but I knew it was good for me, like public speaking. I'd act as if I wasn't scared and then go take action.

It's the same way with money. Act as if you already have the money, and make the precise plans as if it's already in your bank account. The act of stepping toward your dreams makes your dreams step toward you. When I dreamt of going to Paris last year, I thought I had to have the money all saved up before

I could book the flight. Then I remembered this principle. I had enough for a plane ticket so I made it happen, then I received a check in the mail from a piece of real estate I unloaded five years ago! It was enough for three weeks in Paris!

But I really wanted to stay for four months, so I filled out all the paperwork for a four-month visa. It was a load of paperwork but I got the visa so I was prepared to stay just in case something came up, and it did! Many things came up and I ended up extending my trip three times while I was there. Anyway, this just goes to show you that it takes action toward your dreams to make it happen, not wishing and waiting.

There is a lot of room in our consciousness for fantasy lives—things we can dream about without having to actually do the hard work of trying to manifest them. Maria Nemeth, in her book *The Energy of Money*, talks about there being a metaphysical reality and a physical reality, with a border in between them. She said lots of people are having trouble at the border.

Have fun with your dreams, the fun fantasies that make you smile, where you try on the life of a rock star, a movie mogul, or president of the United States. When one of those dreams strikes your fancy so hard that you're willing to do whatever it takes to achieve it, create an action plan and then get to work. If your goal is juicy enough, just working on achieving it will also be juicy! And I think that's the point of it all—choose goals that make life fun now.

Success is not a place you get to—it's a state you live in. If you enjoy the process instead of being attached to the result, you will be a success every day of your life.

Spousal Support

No, not the kind you receive in a divorce settlement—the kind that, when you get it, you don't get divorced!

This chapter is for the husband/father/significant other/friend/boss/employee/banker/politician who truly believes in gender equality. There is support and help you can give and in return receive much support and help from women.

First, I'd like you to imagine for a moment a different reality, one in which the world order is reversed. A matriarchal society is in power, where women hold all the positions of authority and the feminine principle prevails in politics, religion, business, and home.

It might look like this (the following passages are actual quotes from the sources listed except the gender has been reversed):

> For most of recorded history, women have been in power and men relegated to the home. In school, history was taught with a focus on notable women in politics, art, literature, science, and religion. Few men were mentioned in connection with any discovery or scientific breakthrough,

most of the art in all the museums of the world was by women, and all major political and religious hierarchies were dominated exclusively by women. Men were essentially property, having to get permission from their wives to own property, take out a loan, or get a job.

Women dominated the workforce, held all positions of authority in the workplace, and nearly all CEOs and board of directors positions in business and commerce were held by women. Women alone held political power and all of the elected officials were women. Since men were expected to hold the same political values and beliefs as their wives, it was not felt that they needed to have the right to vote.

All the gods were subsidiary to goddesses. In church, you worshipped the Mother, the Daughter, and the Holy Feminine Intuition; all the histories and letters recorded in your holy books focused on the great works of the female prophets throughout history. One of the letters in your holy book says, "Let a man learn in silence with all submissiveness. I permit no man to teach or to have authority over women; he is to keep silent." (Source: Holy Bible, 1 Tim. 2:11–12.)

Some great men started lobbying for men's suffrage and gave their lives for men to achieve the right to vote. The backlash was harsh; most women didn't feel that men had the capability required to have the vote and many men agreed with that position. The female president of the United States said, "Sensible and responsible men do not want to vote. The relative positions to be assumed by man and woman in the working out of our civilization were assigned long ago by a higher intelligence than ours." (Source: Grover Cleveland, 1905.)

But the move for equality prevailed, and men in America were granted the right to vote in 1920. The second wave of masculinism came in the '50s, with Bert Friedan's book *The Masculine Mystique*. It launched the fight to get men out of the home, break through the glass ceiling, and obtain equal representation in politics, equal opportunities in business, and equal pay for equal work.

But still in modern times in America, as recently as 2001, 98 percent of childcare workers, 82 percent of elementary school teachers, 91 percent of nurses, 99 percent of secretaries, and 70 percent of social workers in the United States were men. Eighty-seven percent of corporate officers of the five hundred largest companies, 90 percent of all engineers, 98 percent of all construction workers, and 70 percent of all financial managers were women. (Source: *Women Don't Ask* by Linda Babcock and Sara Laschever.)

Women's sports dominate: women's soccer, golf, figure skating, tennis, and softball get the majority of college funding, national corporate sponsorships, and 98 percent of television coverage. In high school and college yearbooks, 95 percent of sports pages are devoted to women's sports. Local news coverage of men's sports dropped from 5 percent in 1989 to 1.6 percent in 2009. (Source: Michael Messner, professor of sociology and gender studies at the University of Southern California.)

Women and women's values dominate entertainment. Eighty percent of the leading roles are women; when men are portrayed, they are subsidiary characters and subservient to women. Even in children's programming, male characters are sexualized and wear less clothing than female characters. For every one male speaking character in family-rated films, there are roughly three female characters. Crowd and group scenes in these films—live-action and animated—contain only 17 percent male characters. (Source: Geena Davis article in the *Hollywood Reporter* from research conducted by Dr. Stacy Smith at the USC Annenberg School for Communication and Journalism.)

The media says the most important quality of a man is beauty. When a famous talk show hostess was asked by a guest if she could choose between being married to a really brilliant man or a really beautiful one, it only took a second for her to say, "Beautiful!" (Source: Arsenio Hall's conversation with Joan Rivers, during the run of his first talk show.)

I could go on, but you get the picture. I imagine that to consider a world culture dominated by such a reversal of gender norms seems as strange to you as it does to me. I would imagine it feels just as strange to women to consider an alternate universe where women hold the majority of the power, money, and acclaim as it does to men.

I painted this picture to illustrate how we all grow up in a world of differing expectations for men and women.

In my case, growing up in the '50s and '60s, I had the perfect family in the perfect neighborhood—a bastion of middle-class success, puritan work ethic, and family values. All the fathers on our street worked nine-to-five jobs, all the women were mothers and homemakers with no jobs outside the home, and all us kids went to school, played hide-and-seek until dinnertime, then finished the evening with homework. We religiously watched TV shows like *Leave It to Beaver*, *Father Knows Best*, *Ozzie and Harriet*, and the *Donna Reed Show*. They perfectly reflected the world we lived in.

I thought everyone had families like that and lives like that.

My father was a rocket scientist. A graduate of MIT, he designed guidance systems for the space shuttle. He was brilliant and funny, with a terrific wit. He encouraged me to excel, and I loved the look in his eye and the smile on his face when he was proud of some accomplishment of mine.

Years later, I read in *The Managerial Woman* by Margaret Hennig and Anne Jardim that studies showed that in a family where there are no male children, the father will give the eldest daughter the same kind of guidance and thirst for excellence that he would have given his son. That seemed to fit for me, tomboy that I was, playing softball and reading science fiction. I always felt Dad and I had a special closeness.

But something shifted around the sixth grade, as puberty entered the picture, and boys came over to the house to visit. Often we'd play ping-pong on our back porch table-tennis set. I was used to getting kudos for winning from my dad, so when the boys came over, I'd beat them, expecting to be admired for my prowess.

But Dad took me aside one day and whispered, "Let the boy win!"

Dad, who always celebrated my successes and was so proud when I won competitions, was telling me to *lose*? *On purpose*? I was completely shocked. I didn't know how to behave. What had changed?

I thought about this shift a lot, and in retrospect, it was a turning point for me and my future. It occurred to me that although Dad loved it when I was a winner and he encouraged me to be smart and outspoken, that was not the kind of woman he chose to marry. Mom was a beautiful, red-haired Southern lady who could cook up a storm, charm everyone at any party, organize the family, and nurture everyone. These weren't skills I had appreciated until then, and I certainly hadn't learned or practiced them.

As I entered high school in 1962 and then college in 1966, I looked for female role models who were like me. I didn't know any women in business—certainly not female business owners. In 1960, only 38 percent of women worked outside the home, largely as teachers, nurses, and secretaries. Although the school counselors and teachers encouraged us to choose careers that embraced many different fields, there weren't many real-life examples of women who were politicians, corporate executives, news anchors, or doctors. The unspoken expectation was that we were going to college "to get an MRS degree."

I chose to become an actress because it was fun and creative and I loved getting applause. But it was also because that's the only work I could see where women could shine and be the star—and be accepted and lauded for it too. And as independent contractors, they were the closest thing to business ownership I could see. Shirley MacLaine—cute, funny, sang and danced, hung out with Frank Sinatra—yes, that looked great to me!

I landed in Hollywood to begin my acting career in 1970, at the height of the women's movement. Virginia Slim cigarettes had a slogan: "You've come a long way, baby." NOW, the National Organization for Women, countered with a button that said, "We haven't come that far—and don't call me baby!"

With each issue raised by women in the workplace, the lives of working women improved. Today, the gains of the women's movement are recognized—equal access to employment and education, more political involvement, rape centers and domestic violence laws, and laws against discrimination in the workplace. It took thirty years, but Betty Friedan said, "Our daughters grow up with the same possibilities as our sons."

Oprah Winfrey is the world's first black female self-made billionaire businesswoman. Marissa Mayer became president and CEO of Yahoo, and Mary Barra, CEO of General Motors, became the first woman to run a major automobile maker. Sarah Blakely, the founder of the multimillion-dollar corporation Spanx, is the youngest female billionaire.

But they are the notable exceptions. As a group, women still earn only seventy-seven cents to a man's dollar. As of this writing, women only hold 20 percent of elected positions in Congress, but I guess that seems natural, because the majority of our movies and television shows have crowd scenes where only 17 percent of the people are female. As of this writing, only one woman held elective office in Los Angeles City Hall. Women make up a total of 11 percent of tech executives. The percentage of women in computer fields has declined from nearly 40 percent in 1991 to 25 percent today, according to the U.S. Chamber of Commerce, as reported by Rosalind C. Barnett and Caryl Rivers, authors of *The New Soft War on Women*. Their position is that the overt gender discrimination of the past hasn't really disappeared; it's merely devolved into bias—and it's growing.

Who Wins When the Fear of Failure Wars with the Fear of Success?

I mention these statistics so that both men and women can acknowledge the difficulties faced by women in business—especially those who undertake the additional difficulties of becoming an entrepreneur. "Bag lady syndrome" keeps women worried they won't make enough money, but fear of success will make sure that they don't.

When I emailed my subscribers that I was writing this book, a woman wrote me to say, "The fear of failure doesn't seem to bother me. But the fear of success is *huge*. I seem to always be concerned about being so visible that everyone will want a piece of me. Also, they'll find out that I don't really have all the answers or know so much after all. I'll be discovered to be a fraud. But there's a big part of me that knows I'm not a fraud and that I do have knowledge and ideas to share with the world."

Men and women both need to encourage the women in their lives to be successful and to be proud of it. Shower them with praises. Tell them you love them when they win! Tell them you believe in them and to try again when they fail. Encourage women to talk about their successes, because it's easier for them to talk about what's wrong, what's missing, or a mistake they made than to talk about how competent they are or how richly they deserve their success.

One of my clients wrote me a very interesting note about the upsides and downsides of being positive and upbeat, especially when you're doing really well and others around you are not. She said:

> *My husband and I recently had an interesting discussion on making money and having money. We are by no means really wealthy, but we are comfortable and grateful for that. We live in a nice house and have nice things and take at least one nice vacation a year. We make more money than our parents and*

most of our friends. And over the last year, I've begun to feel a little uncomfortable in this area! ...I want to be humble and don't want to brag. But I also don't want to act fake by being careful what I say so as not to be "too positive" or whatever.

In general, I am a positive person, but I worry that I sometimes come off as bragging when I'm just being optimistic—or even just honest. Maybe things are going great!

In yesterday's class, you mentioned that people like it when you're vulnerable or just doing okay. Down and out is uncomfortable for them. Too much success is uncomfortable for them. So my question is—how do I strike a balance with all this? How do I feel okay about doing well and not seem like a jerk to others who maybe aren't doing as well as me/us? How do I stay positive when really that's not what others want to hear?

I feel like I could really skyrocket my wealth, happiness, and all other positive things in my life. That is if I don't limit myself. Have you ever felt this way? I'll look forward to your thoughts on all this.

I understood what she was saying—it is a bit of a challenge to balance feeling upbeat and positive and not coming across with too much good cheer when others are suffering. What naturally happens as some people rise in status, popularity, and financial success is that some of the old friends whose circumstances aren't as rich or happy will drop away, and others who are in your same circumstances will appear. You will naturally attract and gravitate to more successful "dolphins."

When people become richer and more successful, others might complain that they get "too uppity" or "too big for their britches" and don't talk to their old friends anymore. But that isn't the reason their associations change. It's because they are getting different invitations to participate in social engagements and business dealings that used to be out of reach. Sudden fame or fortune can mean many more opportunities than the person is equipped to handle. When they say they're busy, usually it's because they are.

If you're the successful one, it's important to remember that your friends still need love and attention too. That's part of the bargain in friendship. You can't ignore your loved ones while you create a too-busy, rich, successful life without them and then expect them to be there when you finally decide to call a year later. Put them on your calendar on a regular basis. Every dinner doesn't have to be at the Ritz. When you're with people you love, it doesn't matter where you are.

The worst thing to do when a friend or loved one achieves success is to express anger, resentment, or jealousy toward them—that's what drives a wedge in the relationship. Maybe they don't invite you to go with them to Europe for three weeks because they're afraid you can't afford it and they don't want to embarrass you. They will naturally attract people in better circumstances who can and will. But you can still invite them to your birthday party, and they can still come.

Many very successful people want nothing more than to help others achieve success too. When you're the successful one, you can help others by being compassionate and giving support, advice, and help. How did you get where you are? What are the steps you took? Sharing your story of what you did to maximize an opportunity or overcome a difficulty can be very rewarding for both parties. That's why many people write autobiographies and self-help books—they want to help others.

Some of your friends who aren't doing so well will want to know how to improve and are willing to do the work, and they will stay close in your circle. Others won't. It's a natural attrition. No one's life is perfect—you will always have challenges and new lessons to learn on your life's path. The wisdom of when to share what and with whom is a lifelong study that we refine as we age in years and experience.

Don't squelch yourself. You get to be happy, joyful, and rich. You can be low-key about it with family and friends who you know are having hard times, but be sure to find those inner circle friends who are also doing well with whom you can share all the glories too. You're fabulous and you deserve it!

What Kind of Support Do Women in Business Want?

When I got the contract to write this book, I asked friends and clients for feedback about what they'd like to see in it. What kind of support were women in business looking for? What did their partners say that made them happy? That made them cringe? What did the partners wish the women would do and say? What worries you? What's hard about your work and your life? How do you stay balanced? I received some wonderful responses and have included the questions and some of the answers below.

You and your spouse, significant other, family member, or close friends might want to take this survey too. Be honest about what you really want. Then get together and review your answers. Consider this a great opportunity to find out exactly what to do and say to support and help your friend or partner.

Support Survey

1. What do you wish your husband/brother/father/sister/mother/friend/partner/employee knew to do and say to support you?
2. What do you wish they *didn't* do and say?
3. If you're the husband/brother/etc., what do you wish your woman in business would say or do to help you?

4. What's the number one thing that scares you and keeps you up at night?
5. What's the number one thing that helps you and makes you happy?
6. When it comes to money, what's the hardest thing to deal with?
7. When it comes to work and family, what helps you stay balanced?
8. What was your "Aha!" moment that made your business and/ or your life better?

I'm delighted to have opened up this conversation. Perhaps you'll enjoy reading these comments as much as I did. See if you recognize these sentiments from your own experience.

1. What do you wish your husband/brother/father/sister/mother/ friend/partner/employee knew to do and say to support you?

"What to say: anything open-ended, supportive, encouraging. All of those scary moments like 'OMG I have *no* job' that came up when I finally left my agency job a few years ago…with its steady, albeit low, paycheck and its steady, albeit boring, routines… That feeling of 'aaacckk no job!' took a while. My spouse kept reminding me, 'Yes, you have a job; take your time, and it will be fine. You are really good at this, and we can bridge the finances until it levels out.' Those days are long past now, and it is interesting to reflect on that panic on this side of building my business. Currently: occasional support about the pressures of it being 'just me' without staff or a larger organization to fall back on."

—*K.B., marriage and family therapist*

"As you know, I am married to the nearly perfect partner (personal and business) for a successful woman—he surely has some flaws, but I am hard-pressed to find them. He is constantly cheering for my success, never sabotages or downplays my achievements, and roots me on to more, bigger, better. No jealousy ever as he *knows* that I value his partnership and absolutely knows (because I tell him often) that I am more and better with him in my life. When I am in doubt, he does not doubt. He expresses confidence in my ability to sort out the problem and affirms my decisions and choices. When I need his input, he gives it with love and respect."

—L.N., attorney

2. What do you wish they didn't *do and say?*

"Here is what I know when it comes to talking to men about money and business. I have lots of men in my life, mainly my father and my two sons. My sons believe in their crazy mom and trust that things will work out because they always do, so they pretty much leave me alone, but my father…that's another story.

"When my sons were little and I decided to quit my 'secure' but *boring* job to go on my own, my father was not helpful. He continually badgered me about being crazy to do that with a young family! What was I thinking? He kept nagging me—what were my plans? Plans? I didn't have any logical, thought-out plans that would satisfy his analytical mind. His fear for me invaded all his interactions and began to infect my thinking to the point that I had to tell him lovingly but firmly that I wasn't going to talk to him for a few months because I needed to surround myself with only positive and optimistic people.

"As soon as I drew a line in the sand, my own fear subsided, I got a few clients, and when I told my dad, he was so happy and proud of me, and then he said he always knew I could do it! Gee, thanks! I now know not to divulge too much information about my budding dreams to people who fear for my life. I don't need their fear on top of my own!"

—*A.C., travel professional*

"No sabotage, no passive aggressive behavior (i.e., pouting or growling if I am working long hours on deadline). If he wants more time, he is direct and asks for it…and he always gets it as soon as I can give it. He never 'offers' constructive criticism without it being requested. He *never ever* asks me to change anything about myself but supports the things I want to change. Usually, I am my own worst critic, so the things that might bug him (oh, like encroachment of lotions, potions, and creams on his half of the bathroom counter…or those pesky extra pounds) are already on my critical radar. Actually, he helps me love myself more, which is the catalyst for all true change."

—*L.N., attorney*

"Why do women feel that men have certain innate qualities that allow them to be successful in a business setting? Certainly, many men feel that way. Was this too programmed from childhood? In business, consistent behavior, honesty, diligence, and the ability to achieve are the actions that get results. Is that acting like a man? Like a woman? I know my boss in industry decided that women (even though we may have had a MS or PhD) might be honest and diligent but did not have the ability/thought processes to really achieve the results he felt were necessary. Actually he always joked that the MS was missing an R. I am just thinking how much of our made-up stuff has been influenced from very young ages. Such as our limiting perception on money…'money doesn't grow on trees,' 'money is the root of all evil,' etc."

—*B.H., chemist, cosmetics, and coach*

3. If you're the husband/brother/etc., what do you wish your woman in business would say or do to help you?

"My spouse's feedback here: 'It really helped that we gave it a lot of thought and planned in advance so we would know what to expect. We set boundaries and expectations ahead of time. It was really important to address the unknown. I am a planner so that was important to me in being supportive. Another issue was that I have always worked for large institutions and have had a steady paycheck. I have planned a retirement income. It is difficult to empathize with the pressures involved in not having a predictable income. It is not that I don't care or get it—that kind of risk is just completely foreign to me.'"

—K.B., marriage and family therapist

"My guess is that his top requests would be verbal expressions of appreciation, confirmation that I 'need' him, and more of my time."

—L.N., attorney

4. What's the number one thing that scares you and keeps you up at night?

"That I am in charge of every aspect of my business. What if the referrals vanish? What if someone says a negative comment online or in the community and my reputation gets hijacked?… Also, I *am* my business, so what if I get ill? Then what? Typical fear stuff."

—K.B., marriage and family therapist

"That when presented with a complicated problem, I won't get it 'right'—although years of great therapy and sitting at the feet of gurus like you have helped me have a deeper understanding that there is hardly ever a 'right' and 'wrong' when the problem is complicated. I lose a lot less sleep over that one.

"I also lose some sleep over needing to 'win' when so much of every outcome is out of my control, particularly in the field of my own endeavor. Now, more and more, I am satisfied to give it my all and trust that I can handle whatever the outcome is and help my client do the same."

—L.N., attorney

5. What's the number one thing that helps you and makes you happy?

"That I am in charge of every aspect of my business! I love what I do. When I am really busy, it benefits my family directly…not just lost in some larger organization. The satisfaction of a job well done is similar. I am self-motivated. But the sense of my family directly benefiting from my efforts feels very, very satisfying. Also the freedom to know I can follow my own interests, creativity, and strengths to shape my business over the course of time is invaluable."

—K.B., marriage and family therapist

"In the past, I would have said hands down—learning and growing. I also am very happy when I know that I have given something my best effort. As time has wound forward, lately, I find myself happiest when I have made someone smile, given them comfort, or lightened their load, including my clients, colleagues, and friends. I was at a recent event giving a speech about business/personal success and someone came up afterward, thanked me, and told me that something I said changed their life. I still get a huge warm feeling with that memory."

—L.N., attorney

6. When it comes to money, what's the hardest thing to deal with?

"Setting my fees in a way that really values what I provide. Keeping track of fees/billing/finances in the way that I know that I want to and should. Trusting the income stream as stable."

—K.B., marriage and family therapist

"Wanting to give more and staying within a budget. Living large for my husband, and I mean sharing and caring. Sometimes it is hard for me to rein in my inherent generosity to be sure that we are saving for retirement, etc."

—L.N., attorney

7. When it comes to work and family, what helps you stay balanced?

"I am still working on this—year three of my practice has me still more consumed than I would prefer. I will be working on efficiencies this year! Overall it is that I love my family and work very hard to meet everyone's needs—so flexibility is the answer here. My business ownership allows me to schedule how/when I want overall. I sometimes lose track of that benefit, but it is priceless."

—K.B., marriage and family therapist

"My husband is the centering force. By being so fun to hang out with, he is an ongoing invitation to be away from work and doing other things. Playing, even for a few minutes, is a great reminder of how, at its core, life is really very simple."

—L.N., attorney

8. What was your "Aha!" moment that made your business and/or your life better?

"Do not wait until I have it all figured out to get started. Just trust my core skills and the service I provide—focus on doing *that* very well and the details I can work on and refine along the way. Making good, genuine interconnections in my community has also been very important."

—K.B., marriage and family therapist

"There have been so many. However, one of the biggies was how your class cemented a notion that was already in my mind and heart. I had read a *Harvard Business Review* article in the early 2000s on the fine art of saying no. It was written by a woman who owned an executive recruiting firm, and it was how she had built her successful business by serving her target client base well and saying no to people who she couldn't serve properly. She stopped trying to be all things to all people and focused on 'her clients.' When I took your class years later, 'My clients praise me and pay me' already had great resonance, and I started being stronger in putting that into practice. It has served me well, and with very few exceptions (no one is perfect, after all), I am privileged to work with clients who praise me and (promptly) pay me. In fact, just today, I received an email from one of our clients praising one of my employees for being so wonderful in handling his case. This is not unusual and happens to us regularly. Thanks, Chellie!!"

—*L.N., attorney*

Strategies for Getting the Support You Need

Here are my recommendations for strategies couples and families can incorporate into their family activities.

1. Focus on faith rather than fear.

"If you want to make the right decision for the future, fear is not a very good consultant."

—Markus Dohle, CEO, Penguin Random House

You're really not going to be able to accomplish much in the world if you are always thinking "this will never work," "I'm not good enough," "the love of money is the root of all evil," "what if I run out of (money, clients, friends, etc.)." If you spent all your time looking at the downside and what could go wrong, you'd never get out of bed in the morning. You have to look at what you can do to make your dreams a reality and then get busy. Deciding to start each day with a positive outlook is one thing all successful people do.

I encourage every one of my clients to think positively about themselves, their brilliance, their talents, and their businesses. If you and your partner can agree to do this for not only yourself, but also for each other and for the partnership too, your lives will be filled with joy, passion, hope, and prosperity.

Some couples do affirmations together every morning and read from positively focused books like *The Wealthy Spirit*, my page-a-day book of inspirational stories. They report that it helps them to focus on their goals and what they intend to accomplish each day and puts them in a positive frame of mind.

2. Make a list at the beginning of each year of financial goals for the family.

"I've never been a millionaire, but I just know I'd be darling at it."

—Dorothy Parker

It's been said that most people spend more time planning their vacation than planning their financial future. Take an hour with your family to dream what your ideal scene looks like: What do you see yourself doing, having, and being in five years? Ten years? When you retire or come to a period where you slow down and work less? What is your definition of success? What is your definition of happiness?

When you have a financial goal for your business and you and your partner both know what's expected, you forestall frustrated comments along the way like, "So when are you going to start making money?"

It's a fair question, but you'll probably get a better response if it's phrased nicely, like "When do you expect your business to become profitable?" It's best if you address this question at the beginning of the year when expectations can be clearly outlined for both parties.

If, during the year, you see that you are not going to be profitable when you said you would be, you had better have a family meeting and talk about it. State your reasons why your projections aren't being met, what you're doing to change your results, and the new date when you expect profits so that you are contributing to the family's financial well-being.

If you are the saver in the family, don't act like "Mom" or "Dad" and lecture your spouse or otherwise act like yours is the right way and theirs is wrong. This will only make your partner defensive and liable to act out by spending even more money. There's a proper balance to achieve, and if you plan for it, you can both sit together and analyze whether your actions are on target to your goals. Saving money can drift off into obsession too, where you're so afraid to spend money that you prevent your family from enjoying a few luxuries that are easily affordable, given your budget. If you have savings or income that you haven't disclosed to your partner, now is the time to tell them about that.

If you are the spender, look at the larger goals you may be for-going in order to have the things and experiences you're having now. If you have any secret debts or credit cards your spouse doesn't know about, now is the time to come clean and disclose it. Maybe you could still feel you have financial freedom with a smaller allow-ance and more money going toward long-term family assets. It feels wonderful to have no debt and a big savings and investment account. Don't knock it if you haven't tried it.

Savers and spenders need to find a middle ground in which to meet. If the spender can tighten up a little and the saver can loosen up a bit, the family can have a rich and happy life together.

3. Have a monthly budget meeting to determine what happened during the month and set your priorities for the next month.

"There are two kinds of people in life—spenders and savers. Usually, they are married to each other."

—Anonymous

A few notes about two-party budgets:

1. Make sure both parties have a spending allowance that does not have to be reported—everyone needs some money that they can save or splurge without having to be criticized about it. Resist the urge to ask what your partner did with their spending money and you will save a lot of wear and tear on your relationship.

2. In a traditional family, the woman most often takes more responsibility and spends more time on cleaning and child care because they are traditional women's tasks. If both spouses work and the total family income can support it, the family budget should pay for a housekeeper, nanny, or day care. Likewise, the traditional men's work, such as plumber, electrician, handyman, and gardener, can be outsourced. If the budget does not support the outsourcing of these duties, the tasks and time allotted for them need to be equally divided. I suggest you keep a time log for a month and compare actual hours spent at the end of that time. A clearer awareness and more equal division of labor in the home will go a long way toward reducing everyone's stress.

3. For women in business, you need to estimate what amount of income you will be able to contribute to the family budget. This amount will come from the net profit of your business. If you are just starting out and don't anticipate making a profit initially, be honest with your spouse about how long it will be before your financial contribution to the family becomes a reality and how much you anticipate it will bring in. If you expect to need a business loan or working capital from family savings, you need a cash-flow projection that you can share with your partner.

4. Outside of the initial discussion of what your anticipated

annual profits will be, I strongly urge you not to discuss your *business budget* with your spouse. You can't ask your family if it's okay if you buy toner for the copier or an ad on Facebook. These are business decisions that only an entrepreneur can make. Your responsibility is to bring in the money that you declared you would during the original discussion. If you can't meet that projection, then the spouse is owed an explanation of what changed and what you plan to do about it. When you start making more profit than you originally discussed and you can contribute even more to the family finances, that will be a cause for great celebration! Look forward to that.

5. Thank each other at the end of each meeting for the success of your partnership and the love and support you treasure!

Budgeting is a positive process designed to help you make more money and have the life of your dreams. Enjoy watching your fortunes improve, your bank accounts grow, and your debts shrivel into the dust. Celebrate everything!

4. Hire a business coach or fee-only financial adviser.

"A bad coach can tell you what you're doing wrong. A good coach can tell you how to fix it. And a great coach can tell you one thing that will fix five things."

—Orel Hershiser, as told to John Vorhaus in *Card Player*

Having a professional to help you set up your family financial goals could be one of the best investments of time and money you can make. Sometimes it's easier to have a rational discussion when there is an impartial third-party expert to help sort through the issues, many of which are emotionally charged. We all carry attitudes, beliefs, and opinions that may or may not be based in any objective reality but rather passed down from antiquated values that were formed by our upbringings.

Often, we just assume that our partner thinks the way we do and has the same goals.

I once sat with a talented professional couple who were very much in love but at the time quite angry and upset with each other. When they met, they were both working rather high-powered jobs and making above-average incomes. But about a year into the marriage, the woman wanted to quit her job, get pregnant, raise children, and become a grade-school teacher or open a day-care center. Her husband felt completely blindsided by that. "I thought I was marrying a career woman," he complained. "I don't want to carry the total responsibility for making all the income!"

She countered, "We discussed having children and that I wouldn't be able to stay in my job, which has so much traveling involved. I can't believe you would expect me to bear and raise children and work the same sixty-hour weeks I'm doing now!"

You see the problem.

They hadn't talked about their actual goals or made plans for how to accomplish them. Each assumed that their vision of the ideal future was the same one their partner had.

So I asked them if they still loved each other, and they said yes. I asked if they wanted to work out a plan that they could both agree to, knowing that it would involve some compromise for each one of them. They said yes to that too. With that as the beginning, we went through what each of them wanted and needed, what they could live without and what they couldn't, what percentage of the family income each was willing to be responsible for, and so on.

In the end, after three hours, they had a plan they were both happy with and they walked out holding hands.

How much money was that worth?

Most men grow up playing more team sports than women, and

they always have a coach. There's a coach for the football team, the swim team, the track team, the baseball and basketball teams. The focus is on winning the game, risks, rewards, and strategies for winning. In business, men often have mentors who act as their coach—an older, more experienced professional who takes them under his wing and gives them pointers, provides ego boosts, introduces them to other important contacts, and helps them up the corporate ladder.

Women don't get this same kind of training, unless they also play sports. But even then, they play it very differently. My friend Katherine James, writer, actress, and owner of Act of Communication, shared the following.

When our sons were playing soccer, after K-League, the kids were divided into boys' teams and girls' teams. My husband, who volunteered to be a ref, much preferred reffing the girls' to the boys' games. (For obvious reasons, you couldn't ref your own kids' games—that would be an act of insanity, of course.) I asked him why. He said, "Come and see."

What a difference! The little boys all wanted to be hot dogs and to win. Getting them to cooperate and pass the ball to one another was a major thing that coaches worked on. The little girls were all much more interested in passing the ball, cooperating, and working together to move the ball down the field. When our boys didn't win a game, you would have thought the world had come to an end. They were freaked out and angry and generally pissed off. There was a girls' team that season who had never won a single game. *They didn't care. They loved the process of the game and working together. One of the moms said to me, "I guess we aren't doing them any favors by not insisting that they learn that winning matters. Isn't that why we have our sons in team sports—to learn how to cooperate together in order to win?"*

There are no winners or losers playing dolls. There aren't any codified rules in a book. It's about relationships, bonding, creativity, and other aims outside of winning. Girls want to like their playmates. Boys know you need eleven to have a football team, so it's less important that you like everyone on the team. Margaret Mead, quoted in *Games Mother Never Taught You*, said: "We have a belief in our society that boys learn to cooperate with their same-sex peers in games more than anything else." Harragan commented, "This American sex-culture gap seriously handicaps working women if they don't make up for their lack of teamwork experience, because cooperative ability is considered a prime requisite for management jobs."

Unless they have a strong sports background, women are not as involved with coaches as men are. They are also rarely mentored in business. With the lack of coaching experience or the benefits it can provide, for them, spending money on coaching is often a foreign idea. They don't have the same points of reference as men do for these benefits. Sometimes men don't understand the need that women have for the emotional support and educational guidance that a coach, conference, or mastermind group can provide and see it as just an additional unnecessary expense.

One of the women who had taken my eight-week program wanted to invest in my advanced program, but her husband said she did a great job on her own and didn't okay the expense. She wrote: "What's the most frustrating part of all of this is that he balks at the $5k, yet we could really use the totally legit write-off!... The other bottom line: even though it's my business, I just can't spend that amount without him being on board. He's not seeing the value right now, but I'll make him a believer someday."

Because she was the major breadwinner in the family, I suggested that her mistake was in making him a party to the monthly expenditures in her business to begin with. He was not a business owner himself and really wasn't in a position to understand what she needed to buy or invest in for maximum business profitability. Asking him for permission about expenses put him in a bad position and frustrated her when she couldn't explain or convince him. She needed to take back her power in this area and make business expenditures she believed in without running them by him. If questioned about expenses in the future, I told her to say, "This is a business decision that I feel is important to my business."

The bottom line here is that if the woman in business in your life asks you if it's okay to buy something for her business, it's a bad thing.

In the end, she signed up for some additional coaching for less time and less money, so it was a compromise everyone could live with. Ah, the joys of negotiation! Over the two years I worked with her, her business gross income went from around $250,000 to over $600,000.

Many business coaches report similar kinds of successful results with their clients. I'm not saying that all her success was due to working with a coach in general or me in particular. I'm not trying to write the business-coach-full-employment manifesto here. She is extraordinarily talented and already had a successful business when I met her.

But I know there were times when she hit a wall and I coached her past it, when she doubted herself and I cheered her on, when she had an idea and I showed her the flaw in the plan, when she didn't see the next step she needed to take but I did because of my experience. You can't see your own blind spot. Coaching helped her both psychologically and strategically. I know that every time I've taken a seminar or worked with a coach, it has helped me in my business and my life. So if you have the opportunity to get yourself a coach, mentor, or educational program where you get this kind of feedback and assistance, do it.

At one annual awards luncheon for the Los Angeles chapter of the National Association of Women Business Owners, I overheard two women talking about coaching. One asked the other not "Do you have a coach?" but "Who is your coach?"

Business and life coaching is a growing field, and more and more people are getting help from professional coaches, educational conferences, and mastermind groups. Women and men both can profit from these kinds of associations. I would make sure that any entrepreneur's business budget includes this expense category, because it's one that can pay huge dividends. Since women as a group have a documented difficulty asking for what they're worth, negotiating the best deals, or touting their skills and experience, when they learn these skills, it can add thousands of dollars to their bottom line.

It can be the difference between a business that just gets by and one that takes flight.

The Amazing Things I Learned about Business from Playing Poker

"If you bet on a horse, that's gambling. If you bet you can make three spades, that's entertainment. If you bet cotton will go up three points, that's business. See the difference?"

—Blackie Sherrod

Do you have a hobby that makes you money?

As Michelle Anton and Jennifer Basye Sander point out in their book *Weekend Entrepreneur*, lots of people make a few thousand extra dollars a year with their hobbies. Lillian Vernon started her million-dollar mail order business on her kitchen table. Maybe you enjoy baking and could sell desserts as a side business. Perhaps you enjoy picking up great bargains and unexpected treasure at garage or estate sales and could resell them at a profit like the guys in *American Pickers*.

Or perhaps your hobby is just so relaxing and fun that it's a terrific break from all the stresses of your work, like golf, arts and crafts, running marathons or other sports, acting in or directing community theater productions, dancing, or playing games.

Whether it's financially rewarding or just for fun, a hobby can relieve your stress. I have one that is both, and it's playing poker. And it's taught me business skills too!

People often wonder why I like playing poker so much. "You're a financial coach and you gamble?" they ask quizzically.

"And what part of life isn't a gamble?" I retort. "The stock market? Going into business for yourself? Taking a new job? Moving to a new city? Getting married? Getting divorced? You take your life in your hands when you get behind the wheel of a car, jump on an airplane, or just walk across the street."

You're playing the odds every day of your life, calculating the risks versus the rewards of any given action. Putting money in a savings account has low risk but also low reward. Investing in a new business has a higher risk but a potentially much greater reward.

Poker is not only a fun game to play, but it also has helped me develop many skills that are useful in my business. It will help you with strategy, negotiating, reading people, being selectively aggressive, patience, judging the competition, surrendering gracefully, winning gracefully, probability theory, calculating odds, mastering fear, recovering from disaster, and gratitude. In addition, it will keep your brain sharp as you age.

John Kluge, whose net worth was estimated by *Forbes* magazine to be $5.6 billion, had this to say about poker: "If you want your kid to succeed in business, maybe you shouldn't send him or her to business school. Teach him to play cards instead. Card playing teaches you that luck is important, but how you play your luck is even more important."

Ellen Leikind, author of *Poker Woman: How to Win at Love, Life, and Business Using the Principles of Poker* and owner of PokerDivas .com, has a business training female corporate leaders management skills through playing poker. She says on her website that "men and women are different. They tend to go about their business differently—and get judged by different standards—you need go no further than the poker table to see this all in action." She notes that poker is one of the old boys' clubs but that "a woman need not always play like a man to get ahead. She has her own chips, and if she plays them in her own style but with skill and strategy, her chances of success at the poker table and in life [are] very high."

If you can take your seat at the poker table, you can take your seat at the board of directors' table.

It was intimidating at first, to sit down at a poker table filled with men and often being the only woman at the table. But I found that the cards don't care if you're male or female, and I could learn the winning strategies as well as anyone. The hardest part for me was to learn to be more aggressive, and if this is an area you would like to improve in your life, poker will be a great teacher.

More and more women are playing poker now, thanks to some female poker players who pioneered the way, ladies' tournaments that made learning the game less intimidating for beginners, and greater acceptance of women in the poker community.

Because we can play—and win lots of money too!

The Benefits of Playing Poker for Women in Business

Noted poker author Lou Krieger said, "In poker, as in business, the secret is in knowing how to manage risk and capitalize on opportunity."

Poker is a game of skill. It is a game of making correct decisions. As Tony Hsieh, the CEO of Zappos, wrote in *Delivering Happiness*, "Like many people, I had always thought that poker was mostly about luck, being able to bluff, and reading people. I learned that for limit hold'em poker…none of that really mattered much in the long run. For every hand and every round of betting, there was actually a mathematically correct way to play." He included a chapter in his book titled "What Poker Taught Me About Business."

I want women to know these kinds of insider secrets too. The following are some business and life lessons I learned at the poker tables.

1. How to Be Aggressive

Oh, yikes, this was a hard lesson! I was in the "good girl box," remember? I was way too polite and nice, and I was raised not to be "too forward." But poker is a game of aggression—people who take control of the game by betting and raising more often win more tournaments and more money. And guess what? In poker, you don't always have to have the best hand. You just have to make the other people in the game believe you have the best hand or at least doubt their own hand enough that they fold and you take the pot.

The hardest thing I ever learned to do was to bluff and put money in the pot when I had a terrible hand. But in one tournament, I finally tried it: three men checked their hand to me after the flop. It was clear to me they didn't have anything or they'd have bet. When they all looked at me, I fired out a bet, and they all folded. I had nothing. Now that, my friends, feels good! In poker lingo, they call that "betting air."

I often see women fail to be aggressive enough—at the poker table, in business, and in life. When women's lib got all the news in the '70s, they used the wimpy word "assertive" instead of "aggressive" because women didn't want to be "unfeminine" or "come on too strong." Women tell me they "don't want to bother people," so they don't make enough sales calls or ask for the order when someone expresses an interest in their services. They don't ask for raises on the job either. I used to own a business management firm with thirteen employees. Once I complimented the entire team on doing a great job and told them I was so proud that we were meeting our goals. Within an hour, all the men who worked for me had come into my office to ask for a raise. None of the women did that.

Being aggressive, bluffing a pot, and taking all the alpha males' money isn't on the list of approved activities for women—certainly not in the way that a man gets approval and admiration for those things. In business, women will tell me "I'm not in it for the money" or "I just want to help people," which is great if you are Mother Teresa, but not if you're trying to make a living. I think that's why there's still a glass ceiling and a wage gender gap.

An article at PokerNews.com outlined how a thirty-two-year-old former successful poker player named David Daneshgar had gotten his MBA and joined with a couple of friends to start an online flower business. "The venture capital firms we approached actually liked the fact that I had a poker background," he said. "They believed that when the money was on the line, I would come through. They loved the background because a lot of them play poker as well. Having the makeup and temperament of a poker player enables you to weather the storms."

Playing poker will teach you the value of selective, smart aggression, in the card room and in the board room. Take a seat at the table in both.

2. Let Go of Fear

"I must not fear. Fear is the mind-killer. Fear is the little-death that brings total obliteration."

—Frank Herbert, *Dune*

One of the things I notice about women and money is the fear. Fear of asking for it, fear they aren't good enough, fear they don't have enough, fear they won't have enough to retire, fear of their "inner bag lady."

This fear is a habit of thought, which means that it won't matter how much money they get, there will never be enough. I know very wealthy women who are frightened of losing the money they have. Women who don't have so much are afraid they will never get enough. One group thinks, "I hope I don't blow this money and end up a bag lady," and the other thinks, "I hope I get some money so I don't end up a bag lady." Money isn't going to solve that problem. The fear habit will endlessly come up with some "what if" scenarios so that these women will continue to be afraid.

The problem is that when you're afraid of losing, you don't make good business decisions. At the poker table, fear of losing the hand can make someone fail to consider the pot odds and fold instead of putting all their chips in. "You have to be willing to die in order to live," as poker players say. When you're afraid you don't have the best hand or someone is bluffing or you're going to lose—in poker and in business—your face and body language reflect those feelings. Those are called "tells," and experienced poker players and business people know how to read them.

When you decide you're a winner and you act with that mind-set of confidence, you project a tough, smart table image. All the winning poker players have that edge. You never see a timid tuna winning a poker tournament. In fact, in the poker world, losing players are known as "fish."

3. Getting Good at Anything Takes Practice

Dr. Alan Schoonmaker writes some wonderful articles in *Card Player* magazine. He gives advice to poker players on how to improve their game, but I find so much of what he says useful in business too, like this:

> *It won't be easy or pleasant, but self-improvement is hard and often painful work. You'll just have to tolerate that pain. If you're like most people, you can handle physical discomfort better than its psychological counterpart. For example, if you diet and exercise, you naturally accept hunger and aching muscles. You may even say, "No pain, no gain."*

He makes the great point that people love working on things they are already good at, because it feels good. But people hate working on the things that they aren't good at, because it feels bad. "Many people don't realize that they will gain more by working on their weaknesses than on their strengths. They work on their strengths because—at least partly—they enjoy the process," he writes.

I've seen that often with my clients too. The accountants love working on the budgets, but the salespeople hate that part. The people who need the time management class the most often have something come up that prevents them from attending that session. When we focus on everyone in the class telling their story and their goals, the people who aren't good at listening get frustrated. But that's the most important skill to have in sales!

Keeping people on track to learn in their uncomfortable places is the most important skill of every coach and teacher.

4. Patience

I learned patience at the poker table.

As much as I love to be in the action, betting and raising and pushing all-in, figuring out other players, how they play and what they have, moving my chips around, and having a high time of it all, there are times when you are just "card dead." That means instead of great hands like aces, kings, queens, and the like, the two cards you are dealt are a series of miserable looking 9-2, 8-3, K-3, and J-6.

You can't play them, except in certain situations where you think you can bluff. You have to wait for those, or wait for better cards. And waiting is so irritating!

A poker coach once said, "To teach people to play poker, my first lesson would be to tell them to go outside and watch the grass grow for two hours. My second lesson would be for them to go outside and watch the grass grow for four hours." Sigh. When the cards aren't falling your way, you can't make them come. You have to wait for the right cards, right position, or right situation. Trying to make a bad situation work will only get you busted.

I once played in a poker tournament for an hour and a half without playing a hand, but my patience paid off—I made the final table and finished in the money. I thought about that when the economy turned south and the public stopped buying...well, just about everything. So you wait it out, knowing the shift will come. It always does.

Getting frustrated is so easy. And so wrong. It won't make you get better cards. It will tempt you to play badly. It will make you picture the outcome you *don't* want, instead of visualizing the outcome you *do* want. Classic law of attraction. So then you get a pair of threes and think they're aces, overplay your hand, and lose.

This is what people do in business too. They are sending out their ships, marketing their product or service, and getting frustrated when the ships don't come in right away. There's a lull, and nobody says, "Yes, yes, I want to buy that!" They start looking at their bills and getting anxious that they won't be able to pay them. They look ahead and think, "What if nobody ever buys from me again? What am I going to do about the house payment? How am I going to pay for my daughter's braces?"

They start visualizing what they *don't* want instead of what they *do* want. That's when they start doing bad sales, pitching to people who aren't interested, and looking desperate. That's a losing strategy.

People get funny notions about poker when they see it on TV and don't play themselves. They think it's fast, that every hand has a fabulous situation with a full house versus four of a kind confrontation. Of course, in the editing room, they cut out all the boring hours of fold, fold, fold. Most of my life I never had any patience—until I had to learn it at the poker table.

5. How to Read People

Do you have a good "poker face"?

One year, I attended a World Series of Poker three-day workshop with Annie Duke, a world-class poker champion, and former FBI agent Joe Navarro, author of *Read 'Em and Reap*. Annie and Joe met when they were both on a television show investigating how to tell when people were lying. The two of them scored the highest, because in both their professions, being able to tell the difference in how people behaved when they were lying or telling the truth was very important. Isn't that a skill you'd like to have in your business dealings?

When I give a speech, talk with someone, or teach my classes, I can see on their faces if they agree with me—they smile and nod their heads, or they frown and shake their heads. They roll their eyes when they don't believe me, and they grimace when they hit their issue. When I started teaching teleclasses and no longer had the visual clues, I was pleasantly surprised to discover how clearly facial expressions show up in the voice. You can hear the smile in someone's voice on the phone, can't you? Improving this skill alone has helped me immeasurably in my teaching skills and ability to help others.

6. How to Suffer "Bad Beats" and Lose Money with Grace

It's unfortunate, but there's sometimes bad behavior in a poker room. Most people get frustrated when they're losing money.

But most players know that it isn't good for them, the other players, or the game to let their emotions get control. As poker pro Bryan Devonshire wrote in *Card Player*, "It is never okay to berate other players. It's right up there with bullying… If you're a good and winning poker player, you know that it's foolish to make your opponents better or to piss off your customers. If your opponent is a recreational player, then they're there to have fun, and having anybody talk crap about you is not fun. That player will either get better so they don't get berated next time or they simply won't return because the game isn't fun."

If you have an anger management problem, you probably shouldn't play poker. Some of the "injustices" of poker will have you steaming! You wait forever until you get a great hand but someone stays in with a bad hand and wins. Then you "go on tilt" as they say, and in a negative emotional turmoil, blow off all your chips.

One Saturday afternoon, I was playing poker in a friendly game at the Bicycle Casino. Most of the players were regulars and we knew each other, having played the same game often over the past few years.

Sandy, the bleached blond across from me, was a lovely person—away from the tables, or if she was winning. But when she was losing, watch out! Her anger would start to seethe and she'd fling her cards at the dealer and curse angrily. It was a bit uncomfortable.

She was winning for a while and perfectly pleasant, and then her luck changed and she got a couple of "bad beats." She snapped at the dealer, threw her cards on the table, and glared at me.

"Oh, now, Sandy," I said as soothingly as I could. "It's just one hand. You'll have another hand in two minutes and it will get better."

She stopped and stared at me for a moment. Then she said seriously, without a hint of sarcasm, "You must have been loved as a child."

"Why, yes," I said cheerfully. "I was definitely lucky there!"

Several men at the table smiled, and one said to me, "Are you one of those people who thinks the glass is always half full?"

"Oh, I'm just happy if I have a glass!" I exclaimed to laughter all around.

Months later, I saw the guy who had been sitting on my left that day, and he smiled and said he never forgot that I said I was happy if I had a glass. I said, "Sure, because that just means there's lots of opportunity to find something to put in the glass."

"What if you didn't have a glass?" he asked.

"Well, then I'd be looking around at the opportunities for getting a glass!"

Just living my truth, no matter what fish are in the sea.

"That's poker" is the common refrain of poker professionals in these situations. Business owners say, "That's business." You have to be able to recover from your failures, your misses, your bad luck. Luck happens—both bad and good. Roll with it. Getting angry about it will just make you "go on tilt" and blow all the rest of your money. Because you just really don't make great decisions when you're angry.

7. Don't Replay Your Losses

"My friend and I almost won a million dollars," shared Steve, the poker player sitting next to me at the table.

He shook his head with regret and told me his story.

"We were in Las Vegas and this casino had just installed the very first million-dollar jackpot machine. My buddy and I were standing in front of it and joking and talking over what we were going to do next. We planned to sit down at the machine and play for the million dollars and were figuring out what amount we would each put in, when a young surfer-dude type sat down at the very machine we were going to play.

"In only a few pulls of the slot machine handle, suddenly the machine went crazy—lights started flashing and music started playing," said Rick, shaking his head. "He did it—he hit the million-dollar jackpot on the very machine we were going to play!"

"Oh, I'm so sorry," I commiserated. "That must have hurt!"

"Yep." Steve sighed. "It still does."

And I could see it did. Every time he replays that memory of loss, he hurts himself again with it.

Are there losses in your life that you replay over and over again? Life may have hurt you once, but you hurt yourself over and over again if you constantly replay the loss.

Don't replay negative experiences. Find the lesson, learn and grow from the experience if you can, but in any case, move on! Let the past remain in the past, except for glorious winning moments that you bring out frequently to revel in and enjoy again and again.

Poker players are famous for not wanting to hear "bad beat stories." Those are the sad tales of woe about how someone had the best hand all the way until the last card fell, which gave someone else the pot and knocked them out of the tournament. One year at the World Series of Poker, two enterprising young men set up a couch and charged five dollars for people to lie down and tell them their bad beat story. I'll bet they made a fortune.

I don't think anyone is going to let you pay five dollars to tell your business bad beat story. Life has many misses and many hits. I want to play the hit parade over and over, not the sob story. And I want to create new hits too! That doesn't come from the energy of mourning or feeling like a victim.

8. Replay Your Wins and Successes All the Time!

Focus on what you want, and let go of the images of what you don't want. You're creating your future from what you focus on now. If you focus on your losses, you're going to look depressed instead of confident. Dolphins will swim away from you and the sharks will circle. Concentrate on creating new wins—it will energize you to take the actions needed to achieve them.

I love to look at the photos taken when I've won a poker tournament. I replay some of the hands that won the day. I remember the good decisions I made, the hands I laid down because I felt someone else had a better hand, the times I just got lucky when the last card fell my way. At the 2014 LIPS Queen of Hearts tournament, three of us were in the hand at the final table and we all had a straight and were going to split the pot. But when the last card came, it made a spade flush possible and I was the only one with a spade in my hand, so I won it all. That gave me the majority of chips and led to my winning the title. I love to replay that!

Today, focus on winning, treasure, glory, love, friendship, caring, happy surprises, gifts given and received, life and breath, sunshine and rainbows! Put a smile on your face and embrace the day to come, with all its treasures about to be received.

Remember your wins. Expect to win again. Expect to get lucky!

9. Probability Theory and How to Figure Risk/Reward Ratios

This comes under the heading of "know when to hold 'em, know when to fold 'em," as the saying goes. You have to develop a feel for when you're in a good situation to win money or whether you should get up, change tables, change games, or go home. A fellow poker player told me his father, a professional poker player, gave him a great piece of advice. He was losing money and trying to win it back unsuccessfully when his father said, "I think they're going to be open tomorrow." I smiled at that clever way of suggesting he just call it a day and go home. Sometimes when things get too hard, you just have to take a break.

During the years you're learning this, you will encounter three laws:

1. The law of attraction
2. The law of action
3. The law of probability

The law of attraction says you have to believe in yourself and think positively because what you focus on is what you draw toward yourself. The law of action means you have to take positive actions as well as think positively if you want positive results.

So if you think positive and take positive actions, why don't things always work out just the way you want them to?

Enter the law of probability. Probability theory says that if you flip a coin one hundred times, it will land heads 50 percent of the time and tails 50 percent of the time. If you flip a coin only ten times, it might land heads all ten times, but the sample is too small for you to decree that a flipped coin will always land heads.

Applied to business, I see people who will make ten sales calls, get a no ten times, and on that evidence alone decide that they aren't any good at sales calls. They think it's too hard, they don't have any talent for it, they will always get no, and they give up.

I just tell them their sample is too small and to make one hundred calls. Write down everything you say that works and everything you say that doesn't work. After one hundred calls, you'll know what your real percentage is. By the end of one hundred sales conversations, you'll have figured out how to be good at it!

Poker players with math skills have an advantage in the game. If the pot has five dollars in it and somebody bets twenty dollars, there's now twenty-five dollars in the pot—but you'll have to pay twenty dollars to win twenty-five. Not a good bet. Even if you have the best starting hand and the best odds right now, you can still lose, so this is not a great investment of your twenty dollars. The guy who bet twenty dollars has given you "bad pot odds" to call. You want to put twenty dollars in the pot when there's one hundred dollars in it—then you're getting five to one odds on your money.

Many players get caught up in the thrill of the game and ignore the odds. Similarly, it always amazes me how many business owners aren't regularly counting their money and figuring out their profitability on each sector of their business. Poker is a game of making good decisions, and so is business. Use your money wisely, when the odds of success are with you and the possible reward is worth the risk.

10. Don't Chase "Sunk Costs"

In other words, "know when to fold 'em" and "don't throw good money after bad." If you've invested a lot of money in a product or service but you can't find customers who are willing to buy it, you have to let it go. Just because you sunk money into it doesn't mean you have to keep sinking more money into it, trying to get it to work. Once you're clear it isn't working, forget it and move on to something else. In poker, you might have invested a lot of money in a hand, but if you conclude that the other player has a better hand than you do, you have to fold and let her have the money.

For example, I was in a tournament in Las Vegas and had A-K as my starting cards, which is a premium hand. I raised the pot. A friend of mine playing on my left raised again and everyone else folded. Now I'm thinking that if she has two aces or two kings, she is going to be a 90 percent favorite in this hand. If she has two queens or a lower pair, we are in a "race" and the odds are fifty-fifty. Neither option is good for me. I want to test how strong she is before I give up, so I raised her back. She promptly raised again, and I folded my hand. She told me later she had two aces, so I escaped with a minimum of damage.

Had I called because I had already invested a lot of money, I probably would have busted out of the tournament right there. But a lot of players won't give up when they think they are beat. In business, it's the same. If you have a losing business strategy, throwing more money at it isn't going to help you.

Success is a percentage game and it's not a big percentage. An article in *Card Player* magazine by poker pro Dusty Schmidt compared a salesperson and a poker player thusly:

Think of a salesperson working on 100 percent commission. He wakes up every morning with no guarantees. He could go out there and close every prospect he has, or he could get destroyed. There are no guarantees. But he has a certain talent that makes him better than the norm, and that talent shows up every day. If he goes on enough appointments, his talent—his "edge" over his competition—shows up enough times to become statistically significant. It's a numbers game. The more effectively he manages his time and appointments, the more his edge is converted into profit.

11. Be Lucky!

"I'd rather be lucky than good" is a famous poker saying. In poker and in life, you have to take risks and get lucky. I've heard it said that the average millionaire has filed bankruptcy 3.5 times. No one wins every time. But if you keep studying and improving your game, your odds will improve, and you'll win more than you lose in the long run. The main thing is to stay within your budget and have fun.

When I play poker, I try to stay positive and do my affirmations, like "I am a winning player—a powerful winning force surrounds me!" from *Caro's Fundamental Secrets of Winning Poker*. And I try to play good quality starting hands. But you don't win every hand you play correctly, and sometimes you win when you play badly. That's where probability theory comes in, because the profit in poker is in the margin between the wins and the losses (just like in the stock market).

Poker players who know me say I'm really lucky. I've won twelve "bad beat" jackpots in the last ten years, and I know a lot of players who've played regularly for ten or twenty years who haven't even won one.

People in business who know me say I'm really lucky too. In 2014, I was the guest speaker at the eWomenNetwork Calabasas meeting and told them all about positive money affirmations. At the end of the meeting, they raffled off six prizes, and I won two of them! This kind of thing happens to me a lot.

Affirmations are a little secret sauce I like to sprinkle on all my activities. Seems to be working!

12. Use Poker as a Spiritual Practice

A friend of mine sent me an email from Bill Baren, who is a business and life coach. He wrote about his hobby of playing poker and put a spiritual bent on it: "I've created a practice of surrendering control every time I play poker. I practice doing the best I can to get into situations where I have the highest likelihood of succeeding and then I let go of what happens next, knowing that at that point, it's out of my control." He goes on to say that he practices gratitude no matter what cards he is dealt: "When I get two aces (best possible cards), I am grateful. When I get a 7-2 offsuit (worse possible cards), I am grateful."

"This training is carrying over for me into my business world too," he notes. "You can have an amazing conversation with a potential client that somehow still doesn't result in you landing a client. Every day is an opportunity to turn your business into your spiritual practice."

That's a great tip. I've had some wonderful experiences, moments of uplift and spirituality at the poker tables myself. I experienced amazing joy and happiness one ordinary, unremarkable day when I was playing poker. The clatter of chips and the shuffling of cards played background music to the conversation of the players. Now and then, the dealer would call "Seat open!" and a floorman would escort another player to a table. The nine players at my table were all sizes, shapes, and colors. Some were Asian, some Persian, some African American, some white-bread American like me. We were all enjoying the game, taking turns winning a pot, whining a little when we got beat.

A wizened old man who spoke with some sort of European accent was losing a bit more than the rest of us. I named him "Mr. Grumpy" in my mind as he threw his cards on the table with a curse again. "Just take your losses with good grace or go home," I thought primly to myself.

A brash young player named David sitting next to me lost his patience. "Don't throw your cards like that," he lectured the old man. "Mr. Grumpy" yelled back at him, and as he did, his shirtsleeve fell askew, and I saw the tattoo on his arm. A blue tattoo, a number. Like they engraved on you at Auschwitz. Or Sobibor. Or Bergen-Belsen. As he stood up waveringly, clutching his cane, and stalked off, I thought of what horrors this man had seen, what terrors he must have endured in the concentration camps of Nazi Germany.

David hadn't noticed it. He continued to complain about the old man shuffling out the door. "They should reprimand him for throwing cards," he said angrily. "He shouldn't be allowed to play."

"He has a tattoo," I said.

All the players looked at me.

"He has a tattoo," I said again. "Here." I motioned to my arm. "A concentration camp tattoo."

"Oh."

"Oh."

Nothing else was said. In the silence, I could see everyone at the table making an inner shift to understanding, sorrow, kindness. He had a tattoo. We all knew what it meant. And we knew that none of us knew what it really meant.

When he came back to the table, the Chinese man next to him helped him with his chair. The Iranian player smiled and nodded. The old man showed his cards at the end of the next hand he played, and several people said, "Nice hand." I saw David's winning cards as he folded them facedown and smiled at me conspiratorially. "Good job, David," I whispered as we watched our newly discovered friend rake in the pot. A little moment, a little gift, a little win. But I had won something bigger than a few chips that day.

As I threw my own cards into the muck, my focus on the game dissolved; I looked around the tables at the players and saw Indians, Arabs, Persians, Israelis, Koreans, Chinese, and Japanese. I saw African Americans, Jamaicans, Latinos, Swedes, French, Vietnamese, and Thai. Men, women, old, young, sober, tipsy, rich, poor, criminal, virtuous—all were playing.

And in that moment, I saw the tattoos on all of them. Tattoos of sorrows endured and tragedies survived. Tattoos written in invisible ink of courage, of shame, of glory. And all these tattooed warriors sat next to each other, playing the next hand they were dealt in the card game of life.

In that moment, I just loved everyone in the room, and in all rooms everywhere.

And so, sometimes, when someone is cranky or tired or out of sorts, I recall that somewhere deep, in some hidden spot on their soul, they wear a tattoo. They've suffered in ways I am unaware of. They're struggling with issues I may not have had to face. I've heard it said, "Be kind, for everyone you meet is fighting a battle." Yes. We all carry sorrows and wounds from the past.

When I am conscious enough, I smile at them in remembrance of this ordinary day when, for a few brief moments, I knew that and honored them all.

If Life Is a Poker Game, These Are the Rules

(A parody of *If Life Is a Poker Game, These Are the Rules: The Ten Rules for Being Human* by Chérie Carter-Scott)

1. You will receive poker cards.
2. You will be presented with lessons.

3. There are no bad beats, only lessons.
4. Lessons are repeated and learned.
5. Learning does not end.
6. "Hold 'em" is no better than "Fold 'em."
7. Others are only mirrors of you.
8. What you make of the game is up to you.
9. All the answers lie inside of *Doyle Brunson's Super System*.
10. You will forget all of this at the tournament.

Women in Poker Resources

Women have been making great strides in poker over the last thirty years. Talented female players fought for their right to sit at the table with the guys, just as women lobbied for their right to be included in professional associations. Linda Johnson, Barbara Enright, Annie Duke, Jennifer Harman, Susie Isaacs, Cyndy Violette, Marsha Waggoner, and Kathy Liebert are among the women who led the way, won tournaments, earned gold bracelets at the World Series of Poker (WSOP), and popularized the sport among women.

It is interesting to note that Barbara Enright is the only woman so far to have made the final table of the WSOP Main Event. Several years ago, she was interviewed by CBS for a story they were doing on the popularity of poker, but her segment was deleted because, they told her, it was "too positive." Most general media coverage about poker prefers to focus on the people who are "problem gamblers." Poker players know the game is a game of skill. Anyone can get lucky, but over time, the better players will win.

The year 2013 was great for women at the WSOP. Dana Castaneda, a Las Vegas cocktail waitress, won a $1,000 entry fee no-limit tournament, taking home a gold bracelet and over $454,000. Loni Harwood cashed in six different events, culminating in her first-place finish in a $1,500 no-limit Hold'em event for $609,017.

She learned the game by watching her dad play online, and she's just twenty-three years old. Vanessa Selbst won her third gold bracelet in 2014 and is currently the highest-ranked female poker player in the world, with more than $10 million in live poker tournament earnings. On the side, she got her law degree at Yale in 2012.

Men have learned to respect women at the poker table. But since there are still a lot more men than women in the sport, you will have to put up with a lot of advertising featuring scantily clad beautiful women. Google "women in poker," and as of this writing, the first listing you see is "The Top Sexiest Female Poker Players of All Time." Sigh.

Several years ago, I played in the WSOP Ladies' Event and was seated next to an absolutely gorgeous young woman, long blond hair, fabulous body, and dressed to kill. She was a Guess model, and I had to laugh at all the men who crowded around the rail, drooling. Several reporters stopped by to ask for her number so they could set up an interview with her.

"Next life, I want to come back as you," I whispered to her jokingly.

"Next life, I want to come back as a man!" she declared. "Men have all the power."

Well. The best revenge is taking all their money at the poker table while they're distracted.

Women's Poker Organizations

To introduce more women to the game in a friendly atmosphere, several associations and organizations have been started by female poker players. These are great examples of women's successes in the poker business, both as successful poker players and ancillary businesses in the poker industry. In addition, they are great resources for women wanting to try their hand at poker in a user-friendly atmosphere.

Ladies International Poker Series (LIPS)

Lupe Soto started these poker tournaments for women in 2004.

They are headquartered in Las Vegas, and their website is www .LipsTour.com. They offer a full range of events for every skill level of player and are currently in fifteen states in the United States, Canada, and rolling out in Latin America. I love playing in ladies' tournaments—they are just so much fun!

LIPS is best known for the brands Poker Queen Grand Championship, U.S. Ladies Poker Championship, Canadian Ladies Poker Championship, and various state championships. LIPS also founded the Women in Poker Hall of Fame in 2008, honoring women who have achieved excellence and contributed to the industry of poker in a significant way.

The World Series of Poker Ladies Event

The World Series of Poker (www.wsop.com) takes place every year from the end of May to the middle of July in Las Vegas, Nevada. Run by Caesars Entertainment Corporation, it has the largest prize pool of any sporting event anywhere. The combined total prize pool in 2013 for the fifty-five events was *over $200 million*. And it's the only sport in which beginners can play with the best professionals in the game! (Some people take issue with calling poker a sport. As one wag said, "If you can drink beer, smoke, and eat pork rinds while participating, it ain't a sport." Note: nearly all poker rooms in the United States are now smoke-free.)

Held at the same time as the LIPS Poker Queen annual event in Las Vegas, hundreds of women from all over the world come to play in this week filled with women's poker. It's wonderful to meet up with all your poker friends every year at these events!

High Heels Poker Tour

Lauren Failla launched this organization in Florida in 2007 with a clear vision to give women the tools and exposure they need to work their way up the ladder to be the best poker players they can be. The High Heels website (www.highheelspokertour.com) states: "The mission of the tour is to empower women to become champion poker players."

Linda Johnson, Jan Fisher, and Card Player Cruises

I can't write about women in poker without highlighting Linda Johnson and Jan Fisher. They have both been professional poker players since the '70s, are in the Women in Poker Hall of Fame, and together run Card Player Cruises (www.cardplayercruises.com).

Linda is well-known as the First Lady of Poker and has a WSOP gold bracelet. A business owner, she purchased *Card Player* magazine in 1993. Over the next eight years, the magazine grew from a sixty-eight-page, black-and-white newsprint publication into a 132-page, full-color, glossy magazine. As publisher, Linda became an ambassador for the poker world and has cowritten or contributed to three poker books, including *Winning Women of Poker*.

Besides being a partner in Card Player Cruises, Jan Fisher is a founder of the Tournament Directors Association and has served as the tournament director for the highly successful PartyPoker.com Million events.

In an interview I read online, Linda was asked who her most feared poker opponent was. She answered, "None." I love that! Linda and Jan are also two of the nicest and smartest people I know. I've been to a number of their terrific seminars and have been on several of their cruises with my poker buddies. See the sights during the day and play poker at night—that's my idea of heaven!

Poker Gives

This philanthropic organization was founded by poker industry professionals Linda Johnson, Jan Fisher, Lisa Tenner, and Mike

Sexton as a way for poker players and the poker industry to give back to worthwhile charity organizations. The mission of Poker Gives is to raise funds through poker events and private donations and distribute them to mainstream charities on behalf of the poker world.

There's a Lot of Money in Poker— and You Could Win Some of It!

I'd love to see more women winning money playing poker. According to WSOP.com, the final three players of the 2013 WSOP Main Event out of 6,352 entrants were paid $3.7 million, $5.1 million, and $8.3 million going to first place. Although the first- and third-place finishers were full-time professional poker players, second place was won by an amateur, with less than $10,000 in previous poker winnings.

The last woman standing was Jackie Glazer, a professional poker player from Australia. She won $229,281 for her $10,000 entry fee. Women only make up 5 to 6 percent of the field in the Main Event each year, and although many play in other WSOP events, they are always in the minority. The coveted gold bracelet and first place money went to several female poker players in 2013. (I have to tell you what fun it was to see a line of men waiting to use the men's room and there was no line at all for the ladies' room. All us girls had a good giggle over that!)

A lot of people wishing to win the lottery might notice that the odds of winning the World Series of Poker and $8.3 million that year were one in 6,352, whereas the odds of winning the lotto are more like one in 258,000,000.

Have I whet your appetite for the poker world yet? Ready to participate? Good luck! I'll look forward to seeing you at a poker table soon!

Creating a Life While Creating a Living

"Socrates said, 'The unexamined life isn't worth living.' But I say the unlived life isn't worth examining."

—overheard at an AA meeting

What are you working for? What is the legacy you want to leave behind? What do you want to look back and congratulate yourself for at the end of your life?

You may not know the answer today, and that's okay. Your whole life is about figuring that out.

When people ask me how to determine the "right" goal for themselves, not sure which choice before them is best, I just say, "Your best guess for today will do."

Goals aren't about achievement of a dream. It looks like they are at first, but that's an illusion. The joy of the achievement lasts about a minute and a half. The movie stars who win the Academy Awards hug the Oscar, giddily thanking everyone they ever met in their whole lives, and party all night in celebration.

Then they go home, go to sleep, and the next morning, what is it they want?

Another acting job.

They just want to continue their work, their art, their craft. It's the daily doingness—the process of inventing and pursuing their goal—that creates joy in their life. The acknowledgment and applause are wonderful, but they are by-products, not the thing itself. The thing itself is the work—the daily exploration of human behavior, mood, friendships, enmities, glories, and disasters. It's the process that matters in the end. That is what you experience every day. That is what creates a happy person—not the celebration of one moment of achievement of a goal. There is no goal where, when you achieve it, you stop becoming.

The importance of every goal is that it is a path leading you through this existence in a particular direction. You choose the initial direction, but life will take over and lead you on through byways and highways you can't determine at the beginning. Years later, you will look back and, with a sense of child's wonder, exclaim, "Ah, so that's what I was doing there—that's the lesson I was learning." Your job is to pick a path and begin, but it doesn't matter what you choose—life knows what you need and will guide you there.

When I rejected acting because it wasn't nourishing my soul any longer, I took a bookkeeping job and found I loved that. Then I became the owner of the bookkeeping service and enjoyed that. When I saw people got value from my consultations, I started teaching Financial Stress Reduction workshops. Then I started writing books. All the time, I was just "following my bliss," as Joseph Campbell said. I took each next step as it appeared because it seemed logical, felt good, made me money, made me happy, and helped others.

Now, so many years later, I can look back and see the underlying theme—that what most empowered me and made me happy was working with a small creative team to invent a common good that empowered everyone. The thing I enjoyed most about acting was rehearsal. It was the *process* of creating that was enjoyable—after the show was set and we just did endless repetitions of it, I was bored. I had to move on.

The bookkeeping job was with a small, dynamic, growing company filled with happy, intelligent people—another small creative team with a goal to help our clients and ourselves to prosper and grow. The bookkeeping service was the same. Then when I started teaching workshops, I immediately rejected the Tony-Robbins-motivational-big-room-seminar-forty-eight-employee model and decided that small, interactive mastermind groups of eight to twelve people was the way to go.

I didn't see how all those pieces fit together until I looked back at them when I was in my sixties. So don't worry if your life doesn't seem to make sense or your choices are erratic and your goals changeable. You are being led by life to your highest good and greatest bliss.

What feels good to you today? What feels empowering and creative and exciting?

Those are the signposts life is giving you. Go do that.

I Get By with a Little Help from My Friends

Long, long ago, at a networking meeting far, far away…

Well, it really wasn't far away—it was in Santa Monica—but it does feel like ages ago. I went to a networking group founded by Christine Kloser called NEW Entrepreneurs (NEW stood for Nurturing Entrepreneurial Women, or that's what I always imagined it stood for). It was a great group of businesswomen with a spiritual bent that I related to very well.

I met a woman there named Sylvia Silk, who I quickly discovered lived just up the street from me, and we started walking once a week in the park. Sylvia is married to a psychiatrist, has her masters in spiritual psychology, and is just a lovely, deep spirit. I treasure our walks very much and always run things by her when I am confused or searching or mad (angry and/or crazy) about something. Sylvia knows just how to cut to the chase, to refocus my attention on what really matters, or to ask just the right searching question.

During one of our walks, I was very nostalgic. Several of my favorite TV shows, like *Lost*, had reached their finales. Endings were on my mind, and the love and connections between people. I relished the love shared between the characters on these shows and felt a little bereft as they rode into the sunset. I didn't get to share their adventures, struggles, and passions anymore. Yeah, it was all imaginary and vicarious, but it felt like a real loss just the same. Hmm.

A little melancholy, I started down the path of looking at all the losses in my life, all the relationships that didn't last, the hopes and dreams that didn't come true, the plans that didn't come to fruition. That I didn't have a successful marriage, that I hadn't sold as many books as *Chicken Soup for the Soul*, that I hadn't been on *Oprah*, blah blah blah. I was really wallowing in it.

"Chellie, all that is just the ego talking," Sylvia said. None too gently, I might add.

Boom! Instantly, I stopped walking. I looked at her and stopped talking too.

Feeding the ego isn't what this life is all about. The success of a venture isn't the point—it's the *ad*venture. It's the exploration through which we discover our values, vision, and voice. It's the crucible through which we distill our spirits. It's learning, school, soul development. Throughout your journey, you win some, you lose some. Poker players are fond of saying, "The next best thing to playing poker and winning is playing poker and losing." The important thing is to be in action, to be in the game, playing full-out. To learn, grow, love God, love life, and love each other. Oh yes.

I knew that. At least, upon occasion, I have known that. But I often need reminding. It's good that we have people to show us the way, friends on this journey of life, to guide us back to the true path when we stray and get lost in the weeds and bogs of the low roads.

Don't Quit Before the Magic

I was in Las Vegas playing a little penny slot machine. I love the fun of the penny slots—some of them are very clever with their bonus rounds and videos. "China Shores" and others of that type have multiple free games—I once got 983 free games on one of them!

But this machine was not hitting anything. I was starting to get annoyed and thinking things like "Bad machine!" and "I wonder why this isn't working." I was disgusted and about ready to get up and go somewhere else, when I heard a quiet voice inside me say, "Don't quit before the magic!"

I realized I had been practicing negative thinking and immediately switched to "Slot machines love to pay me jackpots" and "I am a winner! I win often and I win big!"

You know what happened? Within two minutes, I hit it for a big win with bonuses and won $635!

Not a gazillion-dollar payoff, but hey, I was only betting eighty cents.

But it got me thinking how many people quit when the going gets tough—right before the magic. I heard a speaker once say, "A road block is just a sign that there's a road on the other side."

How to Stay Up When the Chips Are Down

"The most beautiful people we have known are those who have known defeat, known suffering, known struggle, known loss, and have found their way out of the depths. These persons have an appreciation, a

sensitivity, and an understanding of life that fills them with compassion, gentleness, and a deep loving concern. Beautiful people do not just happen."

—Elisabeth Kübler-Ross

I read biographies of successful people and watch biographical programs all the time. I especially love the parts of how they struggled in the beginning, when they were just one of the millions of unknowns struggling to make their mark.

I used to think that famous celebrities were just so special that they were instantly recognized at their first audition and immediately received recording contracts, starring roles, top positions in big companies. But that almost never happens. Most stars were relentlessly rejected at first. But they weren't going to let a few failures or bruised egos or unopened doors stop them.

As Randy Pausch said in *The Last Lecture*, "The brick walls are there for a reason. The brick walls are not there to keep us out. The brick walls are there to give us a chance to show how badly we want something. Because the brick walls are there to stop the people who don't want it badly enough. They're there to stop the other people."

The 2012 Nobel Prize in physiology or medicine was awarded to John Gurdon and Shinya Yamanaka. According to the BBC, one of Gurdon's high school teachers reported: "I believe Gurdon has ideas about becoming a scientist; on his present showing this is quite ridiculous; if he can't learn simple biological facts, he would have no chance of doing the work of a specialist, and it would be a sheer waste of time, both on his part and of those who would have to teach him."

Ah, the naysayers lurk everywhere on a person's road to success. I think they are really mentors whose job it is to show you that you must toughen up and make your dream happen in spite of them!

So don't be dismayed by the naysayers strewn in your path. They are just obstacles on the road to your success. Climb over them, go under them, or go around them. They are training you to be creative and strong, skills that are needed to maintain a career in anything. Just keep on going and prove them wrong! What was the worst review you ever got? And how did you prove them wrong?

When I was trying to find an agent for my first book *The Wealthy Spirit*, I got a lot of noes before Lisa Hagan of Paraview Literary Agency said yes. What a blessing it turned out to be that all those other people said no! They were just getting out of my way because they weren't my perfect match—Lisa was, and I hadn't met her yet.

Then a lot of publishers turned us down—for a year and a half—before our perfect match, Sourcebooks, said yes. During the turndown time, I bought a book called *Rotten Reviews and Rejections* by Bill Henderson and André Bernard. It was filled with stories of very famous authors' rejection notices, like these:

> *The Good Earth* by Pearl Buck: "Regret the American public is not interested in anything on China."
>
> *The Adventures of Huckleberry Finn* by Mark Twain: "A gross trifling with every fine feeling… Mr. Clemens has no reliable sense of propriety."
>
> *Journey Back to Love* by Mary Higgins Clark: "We found the heroine as boring as her husband had."

Also included in the book was this: "Memo from Patrick Dennis… *Auntie Mame* circulated for five years, through the halls of fifteen publishers, and finally ended up with Vanguard Press, which, as you can see, is rather deep into the alphabet."

They didn't give up before the magic, and neither should you. Be passionate, follow your north star, and the worst that can happen is you live a life full of interesting adventures. It's all good.

The Upside of the Downside

"A deficit is what you have when you haven't got as much as you had when you had nothing."

—Gerald F. Lieberman

There's always something good to be had in down times. There's always an upside, a bright side, a better angle from which to view your circumstances.

Don't you sometimes just get bored silly from all the doom and gloom on the news? I was listening to Jay Leno on *The Tonight Show* one evening at the beginning of the 2008 Great Recession, and he made some really funny cracks about the economy, like, "Did you hear that Ruth's Chris Steak House is giving away twenty-five-dollar gift certificates? That means you can afford the potato." And President Bush had the lowest approval rating ever: "76 percent disapprove of the way he's running the country. The other 24 percent work for AIG."

I just lay in my bed snickering over the silliness. But it lightened me up! So I thought I'd make a Top Ten List, à la David Letterman.

Top Ten Reasons to Feel Good about a Bad Economy:

10. You didn't lose any money in the stock market because you didn't have any money in the stock market. You spent all your money as soon as you got it and got full value for it when it was worth something.

9. You can file bankruptcy with no sweat. They can't take your assets away from you—you don't have any.

8. Sheldon Adelson, owner of Las Vegas Sands Corporation and the Venetian Hotel, lost $30 billion in the last recession. You only lost $30,000—celebrate!

7. People who saved their money lost half of it in the stock market crash. Their 401ks are now 201ks. You never had a 401k. You lost nothing; therefore, you are a winner!

6. You lost your job. But you hated that job anyway. Send your ex-boss a thank-you note and go get a better job!

5. You didn't get elected president of the United States. Whew! It's way too much work, and the press criticizes you no matter what you do. And have you noticed how they all go gray before leaving office?

4. Gasoline prices are back down to $4.30 a gallon. Of course, that's the price that made you outraged last year (credit to Jay Leno for that one).

3. All the stores are now ninety-nine-cent stores. Time for a shopping spree!

2. There won't be any more bank robberies—the robbers are now in the business of lending the banks back their money at 18 percent interest, 38 percent if they miss a payment.

1. You may not be able to afford a gardener, but you're still on the right side of the grass!

So Sometimes You Make Mistakes

This isn't to say we can't learn and grow, that we don't make mistakes. Sometimes I think I've made every mistake on the planet.

These are some of the bad behaviors of which I have been guilty:

1. Getting involved (romantically and professionally) with sharks
2. Having low self-esteem
3. Not asking for what I wanted

4. Not asking for enough money, raises, bonuses, perks, etc. at work
5. Not believing I was worthy of success
6. Not saying positive affirmations (whether I believed them or not)
7. Not taking the good advice of smart mentors
8. Getting stuck in the mud and wallowing in it instead of figuring a way out
9. Continuing to do something that wasn't working because "it's bound to work someday!"
10. Whining and complaining about my life

This is not an exhaustive list. This is just what came to mind off the top of my head in about five minutes. What would you add to the list? Which ones have you done?

Resistance

Sometimes people hit their wall of resistance and want to quit.

I see it all the time in my workshops. They sign up for class and want to drop out when the going gets tough. All their reasons sound so reasonable: their car broke down, their dog (cat, husband, child) is sick, they are sick, they have a new deadline and they ran out of time, they have too much on their plate…you've probably heard a lot of these.

And I should be sympathetic and understanding of their problems, shouldn't I? But here's the truth in one of my favorite quotes by Raul Armesto: "The world isn't interested in the storms you encountered, but whether or not you brought in the ship."

I am pitiless, because business is pitiless. If you want to be in business for yourself or keep a job, you have to keep your agreements, even when it's hard to do. You have to show up for work, even when you don't feel like it. You have to serve your clients, market and sell your products and services, maintain your website, write your blog, post on Facebook and other social media, tweet, go to the networking meetings, pay your bills, save some money, make your house payment, take care of your kids, ad infinitum. Rinse and repeat.

All the excuses in the world won't excuse you from your responsibilities. If you fail to run your business profitably and responsibly, your business will fail.

Listen, everyone has problems. Everyone cries in the night, has a sick relative, is sick themselves, has a computer malfunction, gets overcommitted, runs out of time or money. As the country song goes, "Sounds like life to me." Your job is to manage it.

I didn't always know this. In the very first year of teaching my workshop, I had a woman in my class who was very busy and stressed, and in the middle of class, she asked if she could transfer to the next class. I felt compassion for her situation, and I'm nice, so I agreed. The second time, she had more problems and asked to transfer again. I said sure. But she didn't complete the class the third time either!

That's when I understood the wall of resistance. The problem that stopped her was the very problem that she came to the class to solve, and my giving her a free pass out of the process just delayed her healing. It was wrong of me to do that, and I learned my lesson.

People want to drop out of class when they reach the point of change and they hit their issue—the thing that stops them from having all the riches and happiness they want in life. One attorney friend told me she signed up for my workshop to solve her time management issues. She took my class twice. Both times, she missed the time management session.

So now I have a contract that everyone signs in the first class. I go over it carefully, reading it aloud to them, and getting each person to say "Yes, I agree" to each stipulation. The first agreement is that they stay in class to the end.

But of course, when they hit their issue, they forget all about that. So I gently remind them about their agreement and that it didn't make any allowances for whatever their problem is.

Success takes work. Psychological and physical. If it was easy, everyone would be doing it.

Freaking Out

Freaking out is a natural response to change when it appears negative. Actually, the up and down swings in business are just a manifestation of the standard deviation. You can flip the coin twenty times in a row and always land heads, but that doesn't necessarily mean anything. It could just be probability.

Of course, it might mean that your ships aren't seaworthy, there's a leak in the hull, you've put too much cargo in the hold, or you've hired the wrong captain. Check those things first. But when you're sure everything is in working order, don't pay attention to short-term results. Success is attained over the long haul.

The important thing is to know and manage that in your business. The key to success is to always be sending out your ships—even in good times, when you have all the business you need. But what often happens is that when we have a full practice, we stop sending ships because we're filled up and we don't need them now. We don't want to get too busy and overwhelmed.

But stuff always happens—there's a natural attrition, and some clients always leave. We have to remember the old sales adage "A-B-C: always be closing." You always need to be working to fill your navigational chart with new prospects. If you built your practice up with clients once, you can do it again. Your skill hasn't changed, and there are still lots of people who could become your customers.

What other problems make you freak out—surprise disasters?

"I think my car's been stolen!" my roommate's plaintive voice on the phone exclaimed. She had called me five minutes earlier as she was leaving work and said she would pick me up for dinner. Now she couldn't find her car.

"I'm on my way," I said and grabbed my coat, purse, and keys on the way out the door. I was concerned she was left standing alone outside on a dark street, but I was only fifteen minutes away, and I drive fast.

I spotted her immediately, cell phone in hand, talking to the police department. When she got in my car, she finished the call and said her car had been towed. I drove past where she had parked, and there, in big bold red letters, was a "No Stopping" sign listing hours 7 to 9 a.m. and 4 to 6 p.m. It was right above the green sign that said two-hour parking, but she hadn't noticed it.

"Well, missy, you were a bad girl," I admonished her. She hung her head sheepishly. "And those towing charges are expensive, you know!"

She brightened at that. "It's okay," she said, smiling. "I have a credit card." And off we went to dinner.

A client of mine once told me her father used to say, "If money can solve it, it isn't a problem." True. It would be great if all problems were so easily resolved.

High-Class-Quality Problems

As your life progresses, it doesn't mean you won't have any problems. But the *quality* of your problems will improve.

With a dash of perspective, here are the kinds of fine problems we'd like to have:

- "Oh darn, I have to get new tires on my Lexus SC430."
- "My book only made it to number two on the *New York Times* bestseller list."
- "I can't decide whether to go to the Inaugural Ball with David or Jerry."

- "The electric bill was higher this month."
- "The bakery was out of my favorite cranberry pecan scones."
- "I only made $125,000 this year."
- "I've got to clean out my closet—it's just too packed with stuff."

What can you add to this list?

Procrastination

I read an article in the *Hollywood Reporter* in which they interviewed the screenwriters of the movies nominated for Best Picture for the 2011 Academy Awards. Michael Arndt, author of *Toy Story 3*, when asked, "What's a typical workday like?" responded: "I wake up late, have breakfast, read the paper, procrastinate until I hate myself, and then I just start writing."

Don't you love that "procrastinate until I hate myself"? If I never had a deadline, I'd probably procrastinate forever. But giving myself deadlines, like the ones for producing this book, makes me do what I truly, deeply want to do anyway—speak, teach, and express myself through writing.

When I was in college, I wrote all my term papers in my head on the two-mile walk to campus. I had little pieces of paper in my pocket with a pen, and when I had an idea, I'd write it down. The night before the paper was due, I'd pull out all the little bits, organize them on the table in front of me, and then start writing.

I'd wait until I had a complete paragraph in mind before starting to type—this was in the Dark Ages when there were no duplicating machines and no computers, just carbon paper, and if you made a change on page two you had to type all the pages after that all over again. I hated that so much I wanted to do each paper perfectly from the beginning so I didn't have to waste time retyping. So I wrote the rough drafts in my head and turned in the first typewritten copy.

Now it's so easy to edit, rearrange, and redo a manuscript, I can easily just start writing and go back and rework things later. But old habits die hard, so usually I am thinking throughout the day and scribbling notes to myself on bits of paper. By the time I start writing with my paper bits scattered on the desk, I've got most of the story written in my head already.

Procrastination can mean you're just not ready yet. My friend and writing buddy Carol Allen told me that she observed that my process was to wait until the well was full and then pour it all out. Then there would be a long space of time before the well filled up again.

So if sometimes you don't feel inspired, maybe you're just in the process of filling up your well. I saw Wayne Dyer speak at a conference, and he told a story of seeing the playwright Arthur Miller at a party. Someone asked Miller if he was currently working on a play. He replied, "I probably am."

He was aware that his unconscious was working, filling up the well. So give yourself a break if nothing visible seems to be happening right now. Just make little notes when you think of something and stick them in a file. Before you know it, the file will be packed, and it will be time to start creating.

Just don't make the creating time too close to the deadline! I chuckled at a terrific cartoon by ToothpasteForDinner.com titled "The Creative Process": it showed a long line with "Work Begins" on the left, followed by a very long section labeled "F*** Off." A shorter section labeled "Panic" was next, then a very tiny section for "All the Work While Crying" just before "Deadline" on the right. That was me writing this book!

We Have Met the Nightmare Boss—and She Is Us

"What are you crying about?" asked the Scarecrow.
"Somebody pulled my tail!" cried the Cowardly Lion.
"You did it yourself," said the Scarecrow.

—from *The Wizard of Oz*, by L. Frank Baum

In the spring of 2006, my book *Zero to Zillionaire* was released. Then in the fall, after many months of planning and creating, I upgraded my website and introduced my online subscription-based Dolphin Club. In between these two big projects, I kept up with teaching my workshops three days a week, speaking at organizations, attending networking meetings, managing my hundreds of emails each week, writing newsletters, making phone calls, enrolling the next workshops, writing articles for other groups, doing teleclasses and radio spots, and investigating opportunities for new PR, new websites, and new classes.

At the end of 2006, I reviewed my goals, checked off all the things I accomplished, and looked at the next goals on the list: create the train-the-trainer course to certify others to teach my Financial Stress Reduction workshops, write another book (or two), create a video, record a CD, etc., etc.

Is this list making anybody tired? But you have one just like it, don't you? And many of you are adding children into the mix too!

Aren't we all so busy that our conversations revolve around how overwhelmed we are and how complicated life seems? How all these labor-saving technologies we created have only served to create more labor?

I hit the wall of overwhelm. And I saw that I had become the nightmare boss—the one who says that all you've done isn't enough, that you aren't good enough, rich enough, famous enough, or thin enough. You'd better hop to it, girl!

Wait! I cried. Didn't I go into business to be my own boss so that I could be the dreamy boss I always wanted? So I could take naps in the afternoon, take Fridays off, go away for long weekends, and tell myself I was wonderful and beautiful? Where was *that* boss?

When I had that realization, I resolved to put a succession plan into effect. Like the board of directors of a mega-corporation, I retired the nightmare boss and hired the dreamy boss. I decided that that year, I would undertake no new projects. I would take more time off to play, congratulate myself more on my accomplishments, and reward myself more often. I would award myself Employee Emeritus of the Month and rest on my laurels. And become a living, breathing, human being, instead of a human doing. Ahhh.

So when you don't get your expected newsletter one of these months, remember my dreamy boss is in charge and gave me permission to play hooky. When I don't show up to the networking meeting, I just needed a night off to play poker or go to a movie.

But too much of that, and I get itchy to get back to work. I once ran into Jack Canfield, who was speaking at a very small local networking meeting about his new book *The Success Principles*. I bought a copy, and as he signed it for me, I said, "Jack, you've made millions from the *Chicken Soup for the Soul* books. You get paid tens of thousands of dollars for your keynote speeches. Why are you writing another book, and what are you doing here at this little meeting?"

He smiled, shrugged his shoulders, and replied, "I just have an insane desire to teach."

Yep. I can relate to that.

You Made Up the Deadlines You Beat Yourself Up With

There's an old joke that says, "If you do nothing, your cold will last seven days. On the other hand, if you go to the doctor and take some medicine, your cold will last seven days." The medications are good for relieving symptoms and helping you sleep and feel better, but a cold is a cold and will last how long it lasts. They just don't have a cure for it yet.

This is when entrepreneurs start getting uptight about all the work they aren't able to do. Once when it happened to me, I started getting really anxious that my next teleclass was starting in two weeks and I was missing out on a whole week's worth of marketing and selling, and maybe I'd have fewer people and make less money, etc.—grumble, grumble.

Then I remembered that I had set the dates of the workshops, and I could jolly well move the start date back a week if I wanted to.

Have you ever beat yourself up about not making a deadline when you were the one that set the deadline in the first place? Yeah, that's true craziness.

So I got smart and declared that the next eight-week teleclasses had been postponed one week and would start a week later.

I just pressed my Staples "that was easy" button. Ahhh. I felt better immediately.

That schedule you beat yourself up with? You made it up. So you can make up something else! What would you like to change or rearrange in your life today?

Oh, new projects will come up, and I'll do them—when I'm energized and they look like fun instead of just more work. But for now, I'm busy basking in the glory my dreamy boss is heaping on me for my job well done…

Wouldn't you like to join me?

Scheduling Work and Play

Life is short. Take time off to relax, play, and visit with friends and family. If you truly want to create a life while creating a living, you must do this.

People often ask me about my workshop and teleclass schedule. I teach classes on Mondays, Tuesdays, and Wednesdays.

"Are those the best days for doing workshops?" they ask. "Did you research what are typically the best days and times?"

Nope.

I teach on Mondays, Tuesdays, and Wednesdays because I like to have four-day weekends. So many coaches and seminar leaders have three-day weekend seminars, but I never wanted to work weekends. When you teach in small mastermind group formats like I do, you don't have to make it convenient for very many people. Living in Los Angeles with 20 million people, I always figured I'd find ten to twenty people whose schedules matched mine, you see?

So I always have getaways scheduled on the calendar with my buddies. I love looking forward to them almost as much as I like going on them. As the ad for the Los Angeles Travel Show said, "No one ever wishes they traveled less."

I like to think of myself as a role model for having a fun life. Wouldn't it be great if everyone did that? Yes, I know, some people are going through hard times right now, in different circumstances and different parts of the world. I hope they live through them successfully and find themselves in better situations soon. And then they'll get to have time off to play, dance, sing, and be joyful with their loved ones. Shoot, even when we're going through difficult times, we need to take time off to do that! That's what encourages us to keep going, to hang on, to have faith in the future.

Celebrate Little Wins

I celebrate the little wins: I just got a new client, I made some new connections at a networking meeting, I had a great dinner, or someone sent me a payment. This practice keeps me pretty happy all the time.

If you have to wait for the big win, you're just not going to be very happy in the meantime, are you? I want to be happy all the time, every day.

Marci Shimoff is the author of the *New York Times* bestseller *Happy for No Reason*. In her travels as a speaker and author of several bestselling *Chicken Soup for the Soul* books, she came across very happy people and very miserable people, and their happiness quotient didn't seem to have much to do with their circumstances.

She decided to research happiness, asking everyone she met, "Who's the happiest person you know?" Usually, the first person they'd mention would be someone fabulously successful, but then they'd stop and say they weren't "really happy." She kept searching and interviewing people. She discovered habits that happy people share and determined to write a book to show people how to consciously develop lasting happiness.

I was honored that she chose me as one of her "Happy 100" and included one of my stories in her book. How she found me is quite a serendipitous chain of events.

Marci's coauthor of her book, Carol Kline, had also helped write Jack Canfield and Gay Hendricks' book *You've Got to Read This Book!: 55 People Tell the Story of the Book That Changed Their Life*. I had been invited to submit a story for it, which was subsequently chosen for inclusion.

As Carol and I worked together, we became friends and had great fun sharing ideas and stories with each other. One day, I asked her how I had gotten an invitation to write a story for the book. I knew Jack slightly, but many people knew him, so I wasn't sure he had thought of me for this. Carol said she didn't know, but she'd ask and find out.

She called me back, laughing. Someone in Jack's office was reading another book I was profiled in, *How to Run Your Business Like a Girl* by Elizabeth Cogswell Baskin. They called Elizabeth to ask her to submit a story, and Elizabeth said, "Have you asked Chellie? You have to ask Chellie for a story!" And that's how I got my invitation.

But how had I gotten profiled in Elizabeth's book, you might ask? Elizabeth had bought an early copy of *The Wealthy Spirit* and called to introduce herself and interview me for her book. See how it works? There aren't six degrees of separation anymore. I think we're down to two or three. And they're all a result of sending out ships.

The point is I was chosen to be a role model for happiness because I celebrate little wins. Want to be happier? Find reasons to be happy right now, where you sit, in whatever circumstances you find yourself. Happy without regard to circumstances, but because you've chosen to be. You can always find evidence to back up whatever position you choose to hold.

So today, choose happiness. On a scale of one to ten, ten being best, how happy are you? Whatever number you choose, decide to move up a notch today. What would you have to do to make it happen?

Happiness Can Make You Richer

Psychologists used to just study dysfunction, but recently they've turned to studying what makes people happy. Great idea, don't you think?

An article in the *Los Angeles Times* by Amina Khan headlined "Happiness May Make You More Money" stated, "People who express more positive emotions as teenagers and greater life satisfaction as young adults tend to have higher incomes by the time they're 29," according to a study published by the Proceedings of the National Academy of Sciences.

Studies found that, across the board, no matter what their other circumstances were, happier people earned bigger paychecks. People who were very unhappy generated incomes that were 30 percent lower than average. "The findings suggest that interventions to encourage more positive thinking in kids and teens could greatly improve their future success," said Michael Norton, a behavioral scientist at Harvard Business School who was not involved in the study.

I saved an article written in 2006 by Janet Cromley called "A Chuckle a Day." It had some wonderful statistics about our mind-body connection in response to laughter. Researchers had discovered that laughter beneficially affected the body's hormones. They did a study with a group of healthy men, half of whom viewed a one-hour humorous video of their own selection. The other half simply sat in a room with an assortment of magazines. Their blood was tested before, during, and afterward, and they found that the men who watched the humorous video had 27 percent more beta-endorphins and 87 percent more human growth hormone in their blood.

Previous studies have showed that humor lowers stress hormones cortisol and epinephrine and has positive effects on the cardiovascular system. Blood pressure is lowered overall and the immune system appears to improve. The lead researcher said, "We should become more serious about laughter."

Happiness is contagious too. Mac Anderson and BJ Gallagher noted in their book *The Road to Happiness: Simple Secrets to a Happy Life* that if your friend, family member, or other direct social contact is happy, your probability of happiness increases by 15 percent. If the spouse of your friend, or the boss of your spouse, or some other second-degree social contact is happy, your probability of happiness increases by 10 percent. Having more friends will also increase your chance of happiness, but not as much as having happy friends.

So if you want more happiness in your life, hang out with happier people.

Top Ten Ways to Be Happy at Work

1. Choose dolphins as partners, clients, and employees. It's impossible to be happy when surrounded by angry, whiny, complaining people.
2. Don't overwhelm yourself with too many projects. You can't really be happy if you're tired.

3. Grow rich in a niche. Pick the number one thing you like doing and become known for that, not twenty things.

4. Know your limitations. Not everyone has to be number one; smaller can be happier.

5. Decide that you're already happy and confirm it daily. Make a gratitude list every day of everything you're happy about.

6. Live within your means or create better means. Millionaires have gone broke, so make sure you know how to budget.

7. Watch the news only in small doses. If it's on TV, it's going to be 90 percent negative and depressing.

8. Love people in large doses. People are like thirsty plants—water them.

9. Have a passionate hobby and make time for it. Enthusiastically participate in an activity that is separate from your daily work routine.

10. Have a passionate life and make time for it. Have adventures, opinions, feasts, revels, dances, games, music, operas, museums!

Winning the Money Game

I invented "Campbell Cash" for my workshops and gave each participant a dollar for attending class, doing their homework, having wins, etc. I had pretty green coffee mugs made to use as prizes, with dollar signs, hearts, and prosperity affirmations on them. If they collected at least fifteen dollars by the end of class, they would win a mug.

People jumped into the game of getting as many "Campbell Cash" dollars as they could. They looked for "wins" in their week that they could share in class, they came to class, and they did their homework. People learned to ask for money—they got very creative and kept asking me, "Do I get a dollar for that?"

It built an energy and excitement that carried over throughout the workshop.

But some people had trouble with the homework, missed class, or couldn't think of a win. What was I going to do if they didn't get their fifteen dollars needed to buy the mug on the last day of class? God forbid anyone should leave class without a mug! The first time I tried this game, I was unsure of what to do when we reached the last session.

I asked everyone to count their dollars. As they added up their total, I saw some people looking proud and happy, and others looking a little sad.

I asked Linda in the front row how many dollars she had. "Seventeen," she said proudly. "Congratulations!" I said. "You get a mug!" I turned to Lana sitting next to her and asked how many she had. "Only fourteen," she said sadly. Without the briefest hesitation, Linda turned to her and gave her a dollar.

The whole room breathed a sigh of understanding and happiness. Ah. They knew what to do. The next person had sixteen dollars, got her congratulations, then promptly handed her extra dollar to the man following her who only had fourteen. It continued this way until everyone in the room had enough to win their mug. There was a loving smile on every face and a tear in every eye.

And it has happened like that in every class since.

What was clear to everyone was that each person got one mug for fifteen dollars. If they accumulated more dollars, they still just got one mug. Nobody really had a burning desire for two, three, six, or twelve mugs. The competition spurred them on during the class because it was fun to win and fun to be acknowledged for their success. If they had dollars left over after redeeming their mug, those extra dollars were now worthless to them. But they were still valuable to the people who didn't have enough to get a mug.

No one ever suggested that they would sell their extra dollars or barter something else in exchange for them. Everyone in the group had bonded over the eight weeks of the class, and everyone wanted everyone else in the group to be successful. People were genuinely delighted that they were able to help someone else get their mug. And it didn't cost them anything.

One of the problems in today's world is that people feel they have to bank endless numbers of dollars because they might need them someday. It doesn't matter that they have all they need right now, and they've got their mug. They're fearful of the day they might not have it.

What if they break it or lose it? What if it's stolen? What if they get old or sick or lose their job and can't get another one? So they put away money to ensure their future security. But how much is enough? One million dollars? Two million? Six billion? How much money stays out of circulation as a hedge against imagined future disasters? How many people go without their mug while others stockpile mug upon mug upon mug?

I'd like to live in a society that guarantees every neighbor has at least one mug. Then after that, if you are especially talented and you want to accumulate more, if you like competitive games, you can go for it. Collect ten or twenty mugs. A garage full of mugs. Knock yourself out.

It's fine with me that some people have more than one. It's just not fine that some have none. Women may need to "lean in" to their careers to get their fair share as Sheryl Sandberg says, but business needs to "lean out" and help more people have more. It's possible to change the way the game of business is scored, from who has the most to who shares the most. Is there someone who needs one of your extra dollars to get the prize?

Home

"Home is the place where, when you have to go there, they have to take you in."

—Robert Frost

I was born on June 9. My sister Jane was born on the same day—three years later. Three and a half years after that, my sister Carole was born on Christmas Day. Because her birthday could get lost in the holiday festivities, the family always celebrated her birthday on June 9 too. So we had a major celebration—almost a mini-Christmas—every June 9. A woman once asked me if I resented not having a birthday celebration of my own. I looked at her in surprise. That thought had never occurred to me. The group festivities were always so much fun, I had always pitied people whose birthdays were only single-person affairs.

So it was with great anticipation that I looked forward to one special birthday trip, when my sisters, their husbands, my dad, and I went to Las Vegas for a three-day weekend. We had a great time looking at all the beautiful hotels, shopping at Caesar's Palace, playing poker at the Bellagio and slot machines everywhere, eating a great meal at Hugo's Cellar downtown (topped off with "Happy Birthday" Snickers cheesecake!), and staying up till the wee hours of the mornings.

By Sunday, we were exhausted. We packed for the drive home to Los Angeles, and Carole and I squeezed our suitcases into the crowded elevator. A nice woman in the corner held her hand over the panel of elevator buttons, prepared to push our floor number, and asked, "Where are you going?" Carole immediately replied, "Home!"

Everyone had a good laugh at that. There is no button on the elevator panel labeled "Home." You can't click your ruby slippers to get there either. You have to pack and travel, sometimes many miles and many moons, to arrive back at that resting place of oasis and respite, the comfortable familiarity of home. Home plate, home page, the place of safety where the walls shelter you, the armchair welcomes you, and your people are glad to see you. We set out from home to face each day's unknown challenges and celebrations, and we must dress for the battles of the day. But at home, we can relax, take off our armor, and let our hair and our defenses down.

If you cannot do that at the place you are now calling home, it is not home.

But there is a larger vision of home. Home is the friend you can call in a crisis at three o'clock in the morning. Home is your sense of connection to the moist earth beneath your feet and the beauty of the sunrise; it is the glory of the view from a mountain top. Home is the cat purring in your arms or the dog running to greet you. It is the light in the eyes and the welcoming smile of the stranger you just met who somehow seems familiar and whose heart opens wide to let you in.

The ultimate purpose of work is to be happy at home. The ultimate purpose of life is to be happy. The ultimate purpose of spirit is to help others be happy too. And if we can achieve all that, we will have more wealth than we could possibly imagine.

Sources

Anderson, Mac, and BJ Gallagher. *The Road to Happiness: Simple Secrets to a Happy Life*. Naperville, IL: Simple Truths, 2011.

Anton, Michelle, and Jennifer Basye Sander. *Weekend Entrepreneur: 101 Great Ways to Earn Extra Cash*. Irvine, CA: Entrepreneur Press, 2006.

Appelbaum, Judith. *How to Get Happily Published*. 5th ed. New York: Collins Reference, 1998.

Babcock, Linda, and Sara Laschever. *Women Don't Ask: The High Cost of Avoiding Negotiation—and Positive Strategies for Change*. New York: Bantam, 2007.

Bach, Richard. *Illusions: The Adventures of a Reluctant Messiah*. New York: Dell, 1989.

Baskin, Elizabeth Cogswell. *How to Run Your Business Like a Girl: Successful Strategies from Entrepreneurial Women Who Made It Happen*. Avon, MA: Adams Media, 2005.

Britten, Rhonda. *Fearless Living: Live Without Excuses and Love Without Regret*. New York: Perigee, 2001.

Brunson, Doyle. *Doyle Brunson's Super System: A Course in Power Poker.* 3rd ed. New York: Cardoza Publishing, 2002.

Canfield, Jack, and Gay Hendricks. *You've Got to Read This Book!: 55 People Tell the Story of the Book That Changed Their Life.* New York: Collins, 2007.

Canfield, Jack, and Janet Switzer. *The Success Principles.* New York: William Morrow, 2004.

Caro, Mike. *Caro's Fundamental Secrets of Winning Poker.* 3rd ed. New York: Cardoza Publishing, 2002.

Chouinard, Yvon. *Let My People Go Surfing: The Education of a Reluctant Businessman.* New York: Penguin Books, 2006.

Clason, George S. *The Richest Man in Babylon.* New York: Classic House Books, 2008.

Cohen, Alan. *A Deep Breath of Life: Daily Inspiration for Heart-Centered Living.* Carlsbad, CA: Hay House, 1996.

Dench, Judi. *And Furthermore.* New York: St. Martin's Press, 2011.

Devonshire, Bryan. "Don't Take Life Too Seriously. None of Us Get Out Alive." *Card Player,* January 22, 2014. http://www.cardplayer.com/cardplayer-poker-magazines/66264-justin-bonomo-27-2/articles/21720-don-t-take-life-too-seriously-none-of-us-get-out-alive.

Edwards, Paul, and Sarah Edwards. *Making It on Your Own: Surviving and Thriving on the Ups and Downs of Being Your Own Boss.* New York: Tarcher, 1991.

Garr, Teri. *Speedbumps: Flooring It Through Hollywood.* New York: Hudson Street Press, 2005.

Gerber, Michael E. *The E-Myth: Why Most Small Businesses Don't Work and What to Do About It.* New York: Harper Business, 1990.

———. *The E-Myth Revisited.* New York: HarperCollins, 1995.

Gladwell, Malcolm. *Outliers: The Story of Success.* New York: Little, Brown, 2008.

Harragan, Betty Lehan. *Games Mother Never Taught You: Corporate Gamesmanship for Women.* New York: Grand Central Publishing, 1989.

Henderson, Bill, and André Bernard. *Pushcart's Complete Rotten Reviews and Rejections: A History of Insult, A Solace to Writers.* Wainscott, NY: Pushcart Press, 1998.

Hennig, Margaret, and Anne Jardim. *The Managerial Woman.* New York: Anchor Press, 1977.

Herbert, Frank. *Dune.* New York: Ace, 1990.

Hsieh, Tony. *Delivering Happiness: A Path to Profits, Passion, and Purpose.* New York: Business Plus, 2010.

Kleon, Austin. *Steal Like an Artist: 10 Things Nobody Told You About Being Creative.* New York: Workman, 2012.

Leikind, Ellen. *Poker Woman: How to Win at Love, Life, and Business Using the Principles of Poker.* New Rochelle, NY: Mary Ann Liebert, 2009.

Nemeth, Maria. *The Energy of Money: A Spiritual Guide to Financial and Personal Fulfillment.* New York: Ballantine Wellspring, 1999.

Olen, Helaine. *Pound Foolish: Exposing the Dark Side of the Personal Finance Industry.* New York: Portfolio, 2012.

Orman, Suze. "Time to Act Your Age." *O, the Oprah Magazine.* July 2014.

Page, Susan. *The Shortest Distance Between You and a Published Book.* New York: Broadway, 1997.

Pausch, Randy. *The Last Lecture.* New York: Hyperion, 2008.

Publishers Weekly staff. "Book Production by the Numbers." *Publishers Weekly*, March 23, 2011. http://www.publishers weekly.com/pw/print/20110523/47388-book-production-by -the-numbers.html.

Rivers, Caryl, and Barnett, Rosalind C. *The New Soft War on Women: How the Myth of Female Ascendance Is Hurting Women, Men—and Our Economy*. New York: Tarcher, 2013.

Rowland, Chris, Chris Cosenza, and Bob Cullinane, eds. *Winning Women of Poker: Secret Strategies Revealed*. St. Petersburg, FL: Seaside Publishing and No Limit Publishing, 2011.

Sandberg, Sheryl. *Lean In: Women, Work, and the Will to Lead*. New York: Alfred A. Knopf, 2013.

Shimoff, Marci. *Happy for No Reason: 7 Steps to Being Happy from the Inside Out*. With Carol Kline. New York: Atria Books, 2009.

Shriver, Maria. *The Shriver Report: A Woman's Nation Pushes Back from the Brink*. Edited by Olivia Morgan and Karen Skelton. Basingstoke, UK: Palgrave Macmillan, 2014.

Sivertsen, Linda. *Lives Charmed: Intimate Conversations with Extraordinary People*. Deerfield Beach, FL: Health Communications, 1998.

Smith, Manuel J. *When I Say No, I Feel Guilty*. New York: Bantam, 1985.

Stanley, Thomas J., and William D. Danko. *The Millionaire Next Door: The Surprising Secrets of America's Wealthy*. Marietta, GA: Longstreet Press, 1996.

Twist, Lynne. *The Soul of Money: Reclaiming the Wealth of Our Inner Resources*. New York: W. W. Norton, 2006.

Wilde, Stuart. *The Trick to Money Is Having Some!* Carlsbad, CA: Hay House, 1995.

Ziglar, Zig. *Zig Ziglar's Secrets of Closing the Sale*. New York: Berkley Books, 1985.

Recommended Reading

Ban Breathnach, Sarah. *Simple Abundance*: *A Daybook of Comfort and Joy*. New York: Warner Books, 1995.

Bennett, Sam. *Get It Done: Procrastination to Creative Genius in 15 Minutes a Day*. Novato, CA: New World Library, 2014.

Boldt, Laurence G. *Zen and the Art of Making a Living: A Practical Guide to Creative Career Design*. Rev. ed. New York: Penguin Books, 2009.

Bristol, Claude M. *The Magic of Believing*. New York: Pocket Books, 1991.

Canfield, Jack, Mark Victor Hanson, and Jennifer Read Hawthorne. *Life Lessons for Loving the Way You Live: 7 Essential Ingredients for Finding Balance and Serenity*. Deerfield Beach, FL: Health Communications, 2007.

Carlson, Richard. *Don't Sweat the Small Stuff…and It's All Small Stuff: Simple Ways to Keep the Little Things from Taking Over Your Life*. New York: Hyperion, 1997.

Clarke, Arthur C. *Childhood's End*. Reprint. New York: Del Rey, 1987.

Cutting, Donna. *The Celebrity Experience: Insider Secrets to Delivering Red-Carpet Customer Service.* Hoboken, NJ: John Wiley & Sons, 2008.

Edwards, Paul. *The Practical Dreamers Handbook: Finding the Time, Money, and Energy to Live the Life You Want to Live.* Los Angeles: Tarcher, 2000.

Ehrenreich, Barbara. *Nickel and Dimed: On (Not) Getting By in America.* New York: Henry Holt, 2002.

Eisler, Riane. *The Chalice and the Blade: Our History, Our Future.* New York: HarperCollins, 1988.

Felton-Collins, Victoria. *Couples and Money: Why Money Interferes With Love & What to Do about It.* New York: Bantam, 1990.

Frankel, Lois. *Nice Girls Don't Get the Corner Office: 101 Unconscious Mistakes Women Make That Sabotage Their Careers.* New York: Business Plus, 2010.

Fried, Robert Michael. *A Marketing Plan for Life: 12 Essential Business Principles to Create Meaning, Happiness, and True Success.* New York: Penguin, 2005.

Gallagher, BJ. *It's Never Too Late to Be What You Might Have Been.* San Francisco: Viva Editions, 2009.

Gawain, Shakti. *Living in the Light: A Guide to Personal and Planetary Transformation.* Rev. ed. Novato, CA: New World Library, 1998.

Godin, Seth. *Tribes: We Need You to Lead Us.* New York: Portfolio, 2008.

Heim, Pat. *Hardball for Women: Winning at the Game of Business.* Rev. ed. New York: Plume, 2005.

Hesse, Herman. *Siddhartha.* New York: Bantam Classics, 1981.

Hicks, Esther, and Jerry Hicks. *Ask and It Is Given: Learning to Manifest Your Desires.* Carlsbad, CA: Hay House, 2004.

Hill, Napoleon. *Think and Grow Rich.* Radford, NY: Wilder Publications, 2008.

Jeffers, Susan. *Feel the Fear…and Do It Anyway*. New York: Fawcett, 1988.

Kersey, Cynthia. *Unstoppable: 45 Powerful Stories of Perseverance and Triumph from People Just Like You*. Naperville, IL: Sourcebooks, 1998.

————. *Unstoppable Women: Achieve Any Breakthrough Goal in 30 Days*. Emmaus, PA: Rodale Books, 2005.

Kiyosaki, Robert T. *Rich Dad, Poor Dad: What the Rich Teach Their Kids About Money That the Poor and Middle Class Do Not!* New York: Warner Business Books, 2000.

Korda, Michael. *Power! How to Get It, How to Use It*. New York: Random House, 1975.

Kremer, John. *1001 Ways to Market Your Books: For Authors and Publishers*. 5th ed. Taos, NM: Open Horizons, 1998.

Lamott, Anne. *Bird by Bird: Some Instructions on Writing and Life*. New York: Anchor, 1995.

Laut, Phil. *Money Is My Friend*. Rev. ed. New York: Ballantine, 1999.

Levinson, Jay Conrad, Rick Frishman, and Jill Lublin. *Guerrilla Publicity: Hundreds of Sure-Fire Tactics to Get Maximum Sales for Minimum Dollars*. Avon, MA: Adams Media, 2002.

Mackay, Harvey B. *Swim with the Sharks without Being Eaten Alive: Outsell, Outmanage, Outmotivate, and Outnegotiate Your Competition*. Reprint. New York: Collins Business Essentials, 2005.

Maltz, Maxwell. *Psycho-Cybernetics: A New Way to Get More Living Out of Life*. New York: Pocket Books, 1979.

Ming-Dao, Deng. *365 Tao: Daily Meditations*. New York: HarperOne, 1992.

Molisani, Jack. *Be the Captain of Your Career: A New Approach to Career Planning & Advancement*. Pasadena, CA: Precision Wordage Press, 2014.

Myers, Betsy. *Take the Lead: Motivate, Inspire, and Bring Out the Best in Yourself and Everyone Around You.* New York: Atria Books, 2011.

Orman, Suze. *The 9 Steps to Financial Freedom: Practical and Spiritual Steps So You Can Stop Worrying.* New York: Three Rivers Press, 1997.

Perle, Liz. *Money, a Memoir: Women, Emotions, and Cash.* New York: Henry Holt, 2006.

Pirsig, Robert M. *Zen and the Art of Motorcycle Maintenance.* New York: Bantam, 1975.

Ponder, Catherine. *The Secret of Unlimited Prosperity.* Rev. ed. Marina del Rey, CA: De Vorss, 1983.

———. *The Dynamic Laws of Prosperity.* Marina del Rey, CA: DeVorss, 1985.

Ramsey, Dave. *The Total Money Makeover: A Proven Plan for Financial Fitness.* Nashville, TN: Thomas Nelson, 2007.

Robin, Vicky, and Joe Dominguez. *Your Money or Your Life: Transforming Your Relationship with Money and Achieving Financial Independence.* New York: Penguin Books, 1993.

Robinson, Lynn A. *Divine Intuition: Your Guide to Creating a Life You Love.* New York: Hyperion, 2001.

Roman, Sanaya, and Duane Packer. *Creating Money: Attracting Abundance.* Novato, CA: HJ Kramer/New World Library, 2007.

Schuller, Robert H. *Tough Times Never Last, But Tough People Do!* New York: Bantam, 1984.

Shah, Idries. *Thinkers of the East.* London: Jonathan Cape, 1971.

Shinn, Florence Scovel. *The Game of Life and How to Play It.* Marina del Rey, CA: DeVorss, 1978.

Sinetar, Marsha. *Do What You Love, the Money Will Follow.* New York: Dell, 1987.

Stanny, Barbara. *Overcoming Underearning: A Five-Step Plan to a Richer Life.* New York: Harper Business, 2007.

Tam, Marilyn. *The Happiness Choice: The Five Decisions That Will Take You from Where You Are to Where You Want to Be.* Hoboken, NJ: John Wiley & Sons, 2013.

Travers, Dallas. *The Tao of Show Business: How to Pursue Your Dream Without Losing Your Mind.* Dallastown, PA: Love Your Life Publishing, 2009.

Weston, Liz. *Your Credit Score: How to Fix, Improve, and Protect the 3-Digit Number That Shapes Your Financial Future.* Upper Saddle River, NJ: Pearson Education, 2005.

Williamson, Marianne. *The Law of Divine Compensation: On Work, Money, and Miracles.* New York: HarperOne, 2012.

Index

Acknowledgments

. . . .

"I would like to thank everyone I've ever met."
—Maureen Stapleton, on collecting her Academy
Award for Best Supporting Actress for *Reds* in 1981

I feel like that too! Every person I ever talked with, every participant in every workshop, every client, family member, and friend helped me learn and grow throughout my life. This book is the culmination of all those conversations, trials and errors, wins and losses along the way. I hope that it helps others the way all of you have helped me.

Any book is a collaborative effort. It's a great pleasure to have a page where I can thank all the wonderful people whose contributions enabled me to write this one.

Thank you, Lisa Hagan, my fabulous friend and agent! Every time I told stories to my writers' group about some new and wonderful thing you said or did, they were amazed. "Are you sure she's really an agent?" they asked. "She sounds much too nice!" I loved sending you my chapters in progress because you could always be counted on for many kudos, raves, and a few gentle suggestions for improvement.

And what a blessing to work with Stephanie Bowen, senior editor at Sourcebooks! It was my lucky day when you, Lisa, and I brainstormed about possibilities for a new book to help women in business. You are so smart, and you really helped me order and shape this material. Thank you for every suggestion—your feedback was right on the money every time. And you really know how to give a great compliment too! I appreciated it all.

To Dominique Raccah and all of the wonderful team at Sourcebooks: thank you for believing in my vision and for continuing to support my writing. Thanks to Adrienne Krogh and her team for the beautiful cover, Sabrina Baskey-East for a fabulous job of copyediting, and everyone who contributed. Sourcebooks is a terrific company, and I am proud to be one of your authors.

Thanks to Nancy Sardella and all the members of WRS for helping me build my business, write my books, and learn how to do a decent "round robin." Thanks for showing me that you can make money while having fun and that, as Zig Ziglar says, "you can have everything in life you want, if you will just help enough other people get what they want." You are always the first people to buy my workshops and books and share them with your friends. Any success I have achieved started with you.

Thanks to my sisters, Jane Markota and Carole Wiltfong, and their families—the Markotas: Dick and Robert; the Alwags: Marissa, Max, Maxie, Kara, and Derek; the Poveromos: Lindsey and Chris and his mom Sandy; and the Wiltfongs: Lloyd, Katie, and Nicholas. Family gatherings are always a swirl of smiles and laughter. We are so lucky to have each other! Thanks, Mom and Dad, for bringing us into this world, and we'll see you again one day in the next.

My sincere love and appreciation to my writers' group, Wild Women Writers, Rhonda Britten, Linda Sivertsen, Victoria Loveland-Coen, and especially Carole Allen, my astrologer, who reads and raves and invariably predicts great things. Your loving friendships nurture me, and our lunches/brunches always give me great giggles and terrific ideas.

Thanks to the poker girls: Shelley, Barbara, Bobbie, Rita, Trish, Judy, Amy, Elyse, Debby, and all the LIPS girls everywhere for the happy camaraderie of cards, chips, and chatter. You make life fun! And of course, what happens in Vegas stays in Vegas...

To all the dolphin graduates of the Financial Stress Reduction workshops, all the readers of *The Wealthy Spirit* or *Zero to Zillionaire* who sent me their thoughts and blessings, and all my friends past, present, and future, thank you for sharing your stories with me. I treasure all of you.

I wish you all sunny skies, smooth sailing, and treasure ships in your harbors. Live long, laugh much, and love often.

About the Author

After a first career in musical theater, Chellie Campbell owned a business management firm with thirteen employees for twelve years. In 1990, she combined her gift for public speaking with her financial expertise to develop the Financial Stress Reduction workshops and teleclasses. Designed to treat "money disorders— spending bulimia and income anorexia," she now trains and licenses others to offer her program. Chellie is the author of

Photo by Starla Fortunato

The Wealthy Spirit: Daily Affirmations for Financial Stress Reduction, which was a book of the week on the Dr. Laura Schlessinger radio show and a GlobalNet book-of-the-month selection, and *Zero to Zillionaire: 8 Foolproof Steps to Financial Peace of Mind*, which the American Library Association called "a wonderful reaffirmation of what life should be." She has appeared on numerous radio and television programs and has been quoted in the *Los Angeles Times*, *Good Housekeeping*, *Lifetime*, *Essence*, *Woman's World*, and more than fifty popular books.

Chellie holds a BA from the University of California at Santa Barbara, is past president of the Los Angeles Chapter of the National Association of Women Business Owners, and was the 1994 Los Angeles District Small Business Administration Women in Business Advocate. She has won the Worthwhile Referral Sources Hall of Fame Award and has been voted Most Inspirational Speaker by Women in Management, Speaker of the Year by the Association of Women Entrepreneurs, and Rotarian of the Year by the Pacific Palisades Rotary Club. An avid poker player, she plays no-limit Texas Hold'em tournaments in Los Angeles and Las Vegas and enjoys birding, science fiction, and chocolate. She lives with her roommate, Shelley, in Los Angeles. For more information, visit her website at www.chellie.com.

Praise for *From Worry to Wealthy*

"This is a terrific guide to living a rich life—spiritually, mentally, and physically. Filled with wonderful stories and examples, keeping in mind these principles will help you have confidence, charisma, and cash in your business and in your life."

—Barbara Stanny, author of *Overcoming Underearning* and *Secrets of Six-Figure Women*

"I love it! Chellie put the FUN in fiscal responsibility and education! Chellie's advice has worked for me for decades!"

—Patty DeDominic, founder of International Women's Festivals and former chairman of National Association of Women Business Owners

"If you're looking to master your money and your life, you've got to read this book. Chellie provides fun and powerful financial strategies to take you from anxiety to abundance!"

—Carol Kline, coauthor of *New York Times* bestseller *Happy for No Reason* and *Love for No Reason*, as well as six books in the Chicken Soup for the Soul series

"*From Worry to Wealthy* made me feel confident and capable in running my small business, as well as handling my personal financial affairs. Chellie showed me how to have what every woman needs— money moxie!"

—BJ Gallagher, coauthor of *A Peacock in the Land of Penguins: A Fable about Creativity and Courage*

"This isn't just a book about money; it is a book about how to confidently walk in the world doing what you love without sacrificing who you are. Chellie speaks to the brilliance in us all!"

—Jeanne Michele, PhD, relationship coach

"Our relationship with money is often the difference between our daily reality and the life we dream about. Chellie does a brilliant job providing a road map for mastering the financial tools necessary to lead a life created by you and for you. A must-read—and a gift—for every woman at every stage of life."

—Betsy Myers, author of *Take the Lead*, founding director of the Center for Women and Business at Bentley University, former White House adviser on women's issues, and COO and chair of Women for President Obama's 2008 national presidential campaign

"*From Worry to Wealthy* is a guide to shift your thinking, giving advice and strategy to take you to success, no matter where you begin. A must-read for any business person!"

—John Seeley, bestselling author of *Get Unstuck for Kids!*

"Master financial stress reducer Chellie Campbell has done it again! This book will take you from worried to wealthy in nine fun-filled, entertaining chapters."

—Marcia Wieder, CEO and founder of Dream University

"Once again, Chellie Campbell has written a classic. This book's fun, funny, practical, and cutting edge. I love the reminders and new insights and know my business will be stronger for them."

—Linda Sivertsen, author of *Lives Charmed* and *Generation Green*

"Chellie Campbell is truly the Auntie Mamie of money. In *From Worry to Wealthy*, she takes what, to many of us, is a scary subject (money) and manages to make us feel more alive with possibility than ever before. Her style is so conversational and fun—you'd swear you were having your morning coffee with a girlfriend while getting an encyclopedic knowledge of how to navigate the business world in a way that will lead to the career (and cash!) of your dreams."

—Carol Allen, Vedic astrologer and relationship coach